THE
BOND

THE
BOND

HOW A MIXED BAG OF FOSTER KIDS BECAME A FAMILY FOR LIFE

2ND EDITION

BY A.M. GROTTICELLI

atmosphere press

Thank you to Darren, Charles, Glenn, Melody, Kim, and Andy for continuing to nurture the seed planted by Nina Nelson so many years ago. This is for foster kids everywhere who wish they weren't.

PREFACE

Everyone wants, no needs, to belong to a family: That's not scientific fact, it's natural instinct. Science will tell you that it is the single most important influence in a person's life. However the safety and security this unit provides can be hard to come by and shouldn't be taken for granted. Finding that special kinship is what draws us together and keeps us feeling whole. Especially in today's hectic world, family remains a cherished respite.

Families themselves are made up of all types of people, some biological and some combined through shared feelings of love and engagement. It doesn't matter who is in that family or where they came from, the warm sentiments are the same. However, when you lose that family it's a loss that can't be described in words.

For me the crux is trying to describe what it was like to grow up in a foster care home and my hunger for a family to hold on to. There are many happy endings that prove, when given the right mixture of love and guidance, foster care works. Mine falls in the gray area, somewhere in between victim of circumstance and mental abuse. Disappointingly, my family didn't work. Twice.

This story recalls the tribulations of ten roller-coaster years—1969 to 1979, perhaps my most formative—and what it took to survive the ride in one emotional, self-respecting piece. We were a group of eight kids living in the same house in search of stability: all refugees from fragmented, unloving homes. Circumstances led to heartbreak when it became clear that our domestic dream was not meant to be, at least not the way we envisioned it.

During that time living in Huntington, Long Island, NY, I always referred to Nina and Gilbert Nelson as "Mom" and "Dad," as all of us foster kids had instinctively (and obediently) done under their care. However, reflecting back on an unpredictable cycle of exhilarating highs interlaced with distance, denial, and disturbing lows has changed my perspective. As I was writing this book, I could not get my fingers to type the words Mom and Dad. Instead, I refer to them here as Mr. and Mrs. Nelson. Yes, my feelings of disappointment and abandonment and my sense of being cheated run that deep.

Explaining what it was like to think you were part of a family, only to be "aged out" of the foster care system at eighteen, is not easy. To be led to believe I was there to stay, only to be cast aside was heart-rending. Just like the millions who have (and continue to be) passed through the foster care system in one way or another, it was a journey best left untaken. We didn't choose this, it was thrust upon us.

In describing the bond we formed, I often use the analogy of a group of soldiers enduring a violent battle while isolated in a foxhole. Looking back, only the battle-weary men themselves know exactly what happened. We came from different worlds and were brought together through no choice of our own. Despite the chaos, we hit it off in a way that has endured many tests of time.

1

MY ROOTS

It was just another dreadful day at St. Michael's Home, an orphanage for discarded children in Staten Island, New York.

The sky was awash with the burnt orange hue of a summer day's setting sun, as the fading light peeked through the single, steel-barred, dirty glass window of the communal bathroom. Two counselors held me down hard against an old, well-worn sink as a third methodically whipped my back with a brown leather belt. It was 1968 and I was eight years old. The burly guys on either side of me pulled my hands apart like a tug-of-war rope while their buddy inflicted lash after lash, always with emphasis. Every time the belt struck my back, my chest bumped against the freezing spider-veined porcelain, creating a jarring sensation of pain on my back and shocking cold on my chest. It shot through me quickly and without mercy, like a lightning bolt.

"Give it to me and I'll stop," the one behind me said in a heavy Hispanic accent.

Between hits, I could see his bearded face in the cracked mirror, but I didn't need to. I knew who he was and was very familiar with his bullying ways. I clenched my teeth tighter to brace against the coming pain. And it came.

"Make it easy on yourself," said another. "You don't need it."

"It" was a cheap gold ring with a garnet stone, my birthstone, in the middle. This type of ring was popular with Italian families celebrating their children's official ascension in the Catholic church. My father had given it to me only a week before during one of his too-short, always heartbreaking monthly visits to celebrate my first Holy Communion. Forever thereafter, I would be expected to attend Mass every Sunday and live my life in a good and faithful way. I saw my Communion as a rite of passage, one that I was proud to have achieved.

With all the fortitude I could muster, I resisted their greed. I figured I could take the punishment if I just clenched my teeth and held on a bit longer. I had seen others endure these "lickings" before me. I was fighting for self-respect...and to keep that ring. It wasn't worth more than $25, but it was a prized possession, but not in a religious or monetary sense. That little band of gold represented my dignity, and I wasn't giving that up easily.

I knew the drill. It had been a year since I was sent to this dank, foreboding and physically crumbling orphan factory. For an eight-year-old—or really anybody—St. Michael's Home for Young Boys and Girls was a scary place. Even when the sun shone, a dark fear of the unknown hung heavy in the air, muting its warmth. Nothing felt safe or comforting. There was always a feeling of doom that something more ominous was about to happen at any moment.

In the paltry Long Island City, Queens, neighborhood where I grew up before coming to St. Michael's, I hadn't typically associated with African Americans, Hispanics, Asians or pretty much any nationality other than poor, down-on-their-luck Italians. Here, I was one of just a few white kids. My unfamiliarity with people of color didn't help my confidence. On the outside, I was a tough boy from Queens, but inside I was scared to death. The days were filled with the constant fear of theft or being beaten up, and the nights brought a loneliness that resonated loudly in the still of the dark. Everyone in our group of about 50 seven- to ten-year-olds proved to be either a thief or a victim at some point during the two years I lived there. Many didn't come in that way, but all became changed as a result of the environment. We never knew what each day held in store, but it was rarely good. That was the unnerving part.

The nights were pretty much the same thing. We never knew what was coming, but we knew nothing stayed the same. That was the unnerving part: the "what's next?" waiting. That's why nobody liked being at St. Michael's, but we learned that the best chance for survival was to "take it and keep your mouth shut." Or, more accurately, "keep your head down and you avoid trouble." That meant you didn't do anything to stand out from the rest of the boys. Invisibility was the key to subsistence. You also didn't talk back to your superiors and you made few real friends. The key was to avoid attracting attention because it was typically the unwanted kind.

Indeed, at St. Michael's you were taught to know your place; you were one of many, a group, not an individual. Individuals caused trouble. Disobedience was forbidden and a long list of rules was strictly enforced. We all knew that and mostly obeyed. Like robots or beaten-down prisoners, you stayed-in-line-and-you-made-your-bed-and-you-got-dressed-and-you-took-a-fast-shower-and-you-brushed-your-teeth-and-you-went-to-eat-a-meal-and-you-got-back-in-line; only to do it all over again once you'd finished. The unending monotony was the only constant, and it made you miserable. The orphanage was run with military precision. All fifty of us boys were corralled into separate lines of fifteen to twenty, all doing the same thing at the same time. That's how the place prevented complete chaos.

The kids at St. Michael's were divided up into groups by age, three to four years apart, up to eighteen years old. My group was housed in a large linoleum-floored room filled with rows of beds, each with a wooden locker next to it. The walls were painted lime green, and flickering fluorescent lights buzzed overhead. The only luxury was a small record player that was used sparingly by the nuns to play age-appropriate music when we were all in our beds at night.

If anyone caused trouble or got into trouble due to someone else's transgression (corporal punishment was big back then), the nuns who ran the place would make us sit alone on our beds while everyone else went outside or on a field trip. I don't recall getting into trouble much, but there were a few times I did. After all, I was just a little boy, isolated in a vast room with no one to talk to except the occasional nun or counselor who checked to ensure I hadn't left and escaped outside like others who had tried and failed. I found the seclusion disturbing. Before the orphanage, as a young kid roaming the streets of Queens, I used to like the freedom of being outside, even on a rainy day.

On that specific evening in 1968, while I was taking my beating in that musty, overused bathroom, I was "encouraged" to relinquish that small gold ring with the single garnet stone. As a scrawny kid with no friends (only a series of bunkmates who unpredictably came and went with alarming frequency), I had nothing to show for myself except that ring. This particular beating—executed as always without the nuns' knowledge—was about "voluntarily" giving up that ring to the counselors, who would then sell it. If I let them have the ring, they could tell the nuns it was a gift. I'd seen the very same thing happen to another kid. No one ever believed our side of the story.

Barely able to contain my cries, although screaming never did any good, in fact it made matters worse, I chose to resist this latest attempt to break me. I had relented in the past and given up other things—toy metal cars and a pair of suede winter gloves—but after a year and a half of submitting, it was time to put a stop to it. At the extremely vulnerable age of eight, I summoned a courage I hadn't ever before and decided I was going to take that beating as quietly as possible and not give up that ring. Not then, not ever.

***

I arrived at St. Michael's Home, officially called a "repository for dependent and neglected children" on November 3, 1967 as a skinny and shy seven-year-old. My parents, Concetta and Cosmo Grotticelli, had been continually and violently fighting at the time, and our small apartment was the furthest thing from a domestic safe haven. Amid the loud arguments, my mother got sick and was diagnosed with breast cancer. When the disease got so bad that she had to be admitted to Astoria General Hospital, my father placed three of us four siblings in the orphanage.

Just like that.

No one in his own family really fought him on it or asked why he was giving away his kids. He told relatives he saw it as an opportunity to get back at Connie, although as a heavy-drinking, underemployed piano player, he clearly couldn't handle us by himself. Logic, it seems, didn't enter into his alcoholic brain.

St. Michael's was located directly across the street from Staten Island's largest garbage landfill, and the stench was palpable. We were instructed to avoid staying outside for extended periods of time when the wind blew in our direction. There were so-called "inside days" when the pungent, nose-stinging aroma permeated everything so foully you couldn't breathe the air without risking your health. Even now, I'm reminded of that smell whenever someone spreads mulch on a garden in the spring.

The Catholic Charities of the New York Archdiocese ran St. Michael's, while the Sisters of Mercy over-saw the administration of logistics and activities. Every organization had its "hitmen," and the nuns served the orphanage admirably. Mercy was the last thing those in charge gave us. This was especially true of the counselors. They officially worked under the nuns, but they really ran the place and got away with whatever they wanted.

According to a brochure circulated to indigent parents who were considering giving up their kids, the home was open to "children free from physical handicaps and with intellectual potentials preferably above dull normal." I still have that creepy promotional brochure, which was somehow in my father's possession until the day he died.

Dull normal? Clinical psychologist will tell you that the harsh-sounding term means "having an intelligence level on the borderline between normal intelligence and mental deficiency." Was that how the world saw me? Maybe because I carried my poor Italian upbringing with me wherever I went and that stigma was not a pleasant one to the nuns at St. Michael's. My clothes were usually dirty, my shoes had holes in them and my parents were never around to supervise us so I had few social manners.

"Hey Angelo, where's your mother?" some adult would invariably ask.

"She's at the store," I typically lied, knowing full well I hadn't seen her for the entire day. I too wanted to know where she was. Both of my parents were always somewhere else, most days and nights.

"Tell her you need a new shirt," they'd say.

"I'm getting new clothes tomorrow."

As for being "normal," the streets of Astoria were filled with mentally deficient people—like a kid named Frankie Polito who loved to light fires with a magnifying glass, but always burned his own hand; and Tony Scopello, who would stupidly challenge the older kids to a rock fight. He always wore a baseball cap to hide the lumps on his head.

At five years old, I was roaming the streets with my friends and having what I thought was the time of my life. Breaking rules was our currency. Without adult supervision, life was a series of illicit adventures that might see us busting out windows in the abandoned school building up the block or sitting on the roof of our apartment building at night and gazing out at the city lights. Sometimes we'd jump from building to building, dared to by older kids, and no one ever fell. The worse we did, the higher our profile became among our crowd. We felt invincible and the world was ours for the taking, even if it wasn't really.

But how much trouble could I get into? I was an undersized kid biding time as an unsupervised urchin, roaming the streets during the day and watching TV at night with my older sister, Rose Ann, and, later, my younger brother and sister. Basically, I was a typical lower-class Italian kid from Queens, living in my family's three-bedroom apartment and fending for myself.

If my life was dull normal before St. Michael's, the orphanage was a whole other existence to wrap my head around. Being there meant I had been abandoned, and the invisible shackles of institutional life overwhelmed my spirit like heavy weights. I didn't feel sadness, just an overwhelming disorientation and a sickly sense of moving slowly, as if through syrup. I wasn't free anymore to do whatever I wanted. Pining for my hardscrabble life in Long Island City, I was alone in every sense of the word.

***

My mother was a quiet girl who kept to herself as a child. As a teen, she never went out with friends. And there's no record of her pursuing an education beyond high school or ever holding a full-time job—even before she married. Relatives say she suffered from depression and that might explain why she'd "disappear" for hours. She must have done something to get by, maybe part-time work, since she was certainly not from a wealthy family.

Her parents, Angelina and Michele (pronounced like "Michael") DeRosa originally lived in Jackson Heights, Queens. Angelina was born in Queens; Michael was born in a town near Naples, Italy, and spoke very little English when he came to America in 1924. Like many Italian immigrants of that time, Michele worked hard and stayed out of trouble, receiving his U.S. citizenship on March 27, 1930. With his lack of education and limited English, he was initially employed as a taxicab driver and was barely able to get by. Later, he worked for years at a chemical company that made soap and cleaning products. Angelina often complained about the odor of chemicals on Michele's clothes.

"What's that smell?" she'd ask him every day after work, knowing full well what it was.

The young couple met in Brooklyn in the spring of 1925, married within six months, and later bought a house on 47th Street in Astoria, Queens. After years of saving, they were also able to buy a bungalow in Shirley, New York as a vacation spot to escape the city on weekends and during the summer. Angelina was very religious, while Michele was not. She was so devout, in fact, that she hosted a St. Anthony's Day Mass in her home on June 13th every year. For Catholics, this is the Feast day of St. Anthony and commemorates his death in 1231. A Catholic priest performed the ceremony, which featured a seven-tiered wooden altar built inside the DeRosa living room and strewn with bread and flowers on alternating steps leading up to a large statue of St. Anthony. The event typically attracted about thirty people, which was quite impressive, not to mention crowded, for a small house in Queens.

Angelina and Michele had two daughters—Concetta, who was born November 4, 1927 and Marietta (Mary), born two years later. An earlier child, also named Concetta, died before she was a year old. Perhaps to overcome their grief, the young couple also named my mother Concetta.

Michele DeRosa died of a heart attack in June 1960, literally minutes after chopping down a dying locust tree in the front yard of the bungalow. I was born six months earlier, on January 20, 1960, at Astoria General Hospital, and was given "Michael" as my middle name. I don't remember my grandfather, but I'm told he liked holding me as a young baby the few times my father brought me around. Angelina outlived her husband by twenty years, working as an aide at the same hospital until she died on October 18, 1993.

It was in 1954 that Angelina urged her daughter Connie, a decided loner at age twenty-seven, to attend the annual New Year's Eve party given by the hospital for its employees at a nightclub in Astoria. The story goes that Angelina bought Connie a dark blue dress (that Connie didn't like), hastily applied makeup on Connie's face, and literally walked her to the party. That night Connie—again after much prompting from my grandmother—met the friendly, slightly attractive Italian fellow playing the piano. His name was Cosmo Thomas Grotticelli. They were married a year later, on January 9, 1955, in Queens, and my sister Rose Ann was born that Christmas Eve.

Connie liked to tell people she was enamored of celebrities. That's why, it's said, she was initially attracted to Cosmo. Apparently, being on stage playing piano in a local orchestra was "famous" in her eyes.

Most people called Cosmo "Gus." He came from a gregarious Italian family headed by Arcangelo Grotticelli and Rosalia Savatteri, who had two boys and five girls. Cosmo, the youngest, grew up in Brooklyn and later served as an assistant medic in the U.S Army, private first class, during World War II.

After the war, he earned a degree in music theory and considered teaching as a profession. Instead, he played at family gatherings, and in nightclubs and music halls throughout New York City. His sisters loved his piano playing and his animated style of manipulating the keys. They all had a favorite song and he knew them all off the top of his head. After dinner the table would be moved aside and they would dance and he played for hours.

One night while playing at a local club, a representative for Guy Lombardo's band saw him and soon Gus was playing piano in Lombardo's orchestra. He later played for Louis Prima's band at several live and radio events but didn't last a year. He was fired after a drunken argument with the famous bandleader.

My parents' stormy marriage eventually produced four children. I (Angelo Michael) followed Rose Ann on

January 20, 1960; Charles Thomas came on July 8, 1964; and our sister Mary Theresa was the last, arriving on February 14, 1966. My mother couldn't figure out what to call the new baby, so that task fell to Rose Ann.

"I don't know what her name should be," Connie said, lying in a recovery room with a new baby girl on her chest. It seemed an odd thing to say. Parents should know what to call their babies.

I remember standing close to her bed at Astoria General Hospital with Rose Ann. There were nurses bustling around us in every direction and there were at least three other women in the same recovery room. It was hot and the staff kept telling me to move away from the bed and give my mom room to breathe. I was calling the other babies ugly, which made Rose Ann mad. I didn't care. I had a new sister and my leg was uncontrollably moving with excitement.

"Stop shaking the bed," Rose Ann scolded, acting bossy and superior like she always did back then. "You'll scramble the baby's brain."

My father was there as well but lingered off to the side. With and he and Connie not getting along at all at this point, he didn't share my joy. After naming Charles and me after his family ancestors who came before him, Gus had no interest whatsoever in the little baby girl. She was another mouth to feed. It's even possible that Mary Theresa was an unwanted accident. However, there was still a birth certificate to fill out.

"You name her," Connie told Rose Ann. "After three kids, I've run out of ideas."

My mother seemed defeated in this moment, clearly overwhelmed by the burden of it all. My father had been out drinking the night before, as she went into labor, and came back in the morning, about an hour after the baby was born with us kids in tow.

And so it was that my newborn sister was given two first names, like Rose Ann, who felt so proud of herself afterward. She loved being in control.

"I got to name the baby and you didn't," she teased me. "That means I'm more special."

As a precocious six-year-old, I didn't really care, but Rose Ann seemed to relish her newfound maternal role. Once the baby came home, Rose Ann treated her like her own, changing diapers, warming milk bottles (when there was milk to be had) and babysitting when my mother went out, which was often. At ten years old, Rose Ann wasn't much more than a baby herself, but only my grandmother questioned the sense of it, often deriding Connie's mother-ly skills.

"What kind of mother leaves her kids alone with no food in the house," she'd say. "I was home with you every day."

It was indeed true that we often ate ketchup on bread to quell our hunger pains. This was actually Rose Ann's idea, and the rest of us kids heartily embraced it. We called them "wish sandwiches." We'd take a bite, then wish really hard that there was something else inside.

When we weren't eating wish sandwiches, we bought sandwiches on credit from the local delicatessen. My childhood friend, Thomas Murphy, and I stole empty soda bottles from the delivery truck out front, and then ran back into the store to get the deposit money, which we'd then spend on food; for me it was most often bologna and American cheese heroes. And candy.

In 1955, Cosmo had listed his occupation on Rose Ann's birth certificate as "piano player." As his musician's income was unpredictable at best, money (or the lack thereof) was always an issue. By the time Charles was born, eight years later, Cosmo had taken a daytime job clerking at an insurance company to help make ends meet.

Looking back today, it's clear Connie and Cosmo were ill-suited for each other. When they weren't arguing, they spent most of their time apart: she visiting relatives or other men and he drinking and playing piano in a local club or at a wedding.

The awkward-together newlyweds raised their children in Long Island City, first on 30th Avenue and later in a second-floor apartment on 9th Street. It caused Cosmo much personal frustration (which he confessed to me later in life) that his skillful piano playing was relegated to small clubs and bars. However, being a drinker limited his opportunities and he could rarely put two nickels together.

***

With our parents often out and about, Rose Ann and I raised Charles and my younger sister, Mary, by ourselves. To help pass the time, I'd build makeshift forts out of blankets in the living room and make up funny songs to keep our younger siblings entertained. I changed Charles's cloth diapers when I was only five years old. I wasn't taught how. I just did what Rose Ann did, then did it myself as quickly as possible.

As a baby, Charles cried for hours on end. Rose Ann and I once put toilet paper in our ears to drown out the sound of his wailing. One time, Rose Ann put paper in

Mary's ears, too, to help her sleep. We tried everything to get Charles to stop crying. The only thing that worked was warm milk, and we never seemed to have enough of that.

I cut Charles's hair when he was a baby, although to this day I blame the local barber. I had made friends with Anthony, a gruff man in his sixties who smoked cigars while he cut hair. He had a barbershop down the street and most afternoons after school, I'd sit in an empty chair and watch him work. I also got free haircuts. Cutting hair was just something I saw Anthony do every day. If he could do it, so could I.

When my father came home that night and saw what I'd done, he gave me a serious beating, yelling for all the neighbors to hear that I could have killed my baby brother. Later, while I was sobbing in my room, the same room where Charles's crib was, my mother came in and said she thought the baby's haircut looked nice. I secretly felt proud of what I had done, although I can't swear that Charles's few remaining bangs were straight.

Rose Ann had her own issues. Most girls played with dolls; she would carry on hours-long conversations with a broom. I would hear her talking loudly and when I'd walk into her room, she'd be holding a broom head up to her face and lecturing it or joking with it. It was her imaginary friend, but it always gave me the creeps because she took those pretend conversations very seriously.

At five years old, I was growing up fast. I had to. As anyone who lived in Long Island City, Queens in the early 1960s will tell you, it was a gritty existence, filled with long boring days of hanging out and collecting random things in the street just for the fun of it. I dreamed of living in the great outdoors but it was so far away, coming alive in pictures and on TV.

So, we found things to do amid our concrete jungle. My friends and I would challenge each other in the morning to see who could pick up the most bottle caps on the street. Then we'd separate, coming back together to compare our bounty at the end of the afternoon. The caps were given (sometimes sold) to older kids who would melt crayons into them and then use them in a street game called Knockout.

Once while looking for paperclips, and finding hundreds, I unexpectedly found a newly hatched chick in the street that had fallen out of its nest. Wildlife was an unfamiliar concept—to me, it meant cats and dogs. The little bird had no feathers, couldn't walk or fly, and was squeaking for food. It was helpless, afraid, and, like me, needed a savior. I took it home and tried to raise it in the bathtub, but it wouldn't eat the breadcrumbs I force-fed it and died within two days. Strangely, I wasn't upset about the bird's death. The streets of Astoria had installed a numbness to truly caring about anything. There were callouses where my empathy should have been. For me, this bird was just another meaningless yet interesting thing discarded in the street.

The day it died I threw the small lifeless chick in the garbage and continued on looking in the streets, curbs, and empty lots for other meaningless yet interesting thing things. Winning the collecting challenge mattered more.

There was no such thing as wide-open spaces or fresh air. Ours was a stagnant concrete environment that we, even at a young age, instinctively learned to navigate with a survivor mentality. Because virtually everyone in the neighborhood was poor, you ate when you could find something edible and picked up old discarded sneakers from the trash and put them right on (assuming they were within two sizes of your feet).

That's what everyone I knew did, so that's what I did, too. Consequently, I grew up fast. The weight of the humid summer air, like the dampness of the cold winter nights, slowed everything down, it seemed, and affected everyone. Nobody I knew had air conditioning, just large noisy fans that blasted from every open window. Our only reprieve was the *Mister Softee* ice cream truck that came by every afternoon. There was no mistaking the telltale music of the theme song and how it grabbed our attention as soon as we heard its siren's call. When I heard it, I'd asked to borrow money from some adult (either related to you or not) and run out into the street to be the first in line. One time the ice cream truck hit a kid, who quickly stood up, demanded a free soft cone, and got one. My friend Thomas saw it happen and the next day tried to fake an accident to get a free ice cream, but the driver saw the whole thing in his side mirror. He kicked Thomas in the ass and sent us both running away. The guy couldn't have been too upset, though, because he sold us ice cream again the next day.

We also had the "Half Moon," an amusement ride familiar to everyone who grew up in Queens in the fifties and sixties. This particularly unsafe kids' ride consisted of an old flatbed truck with a semicircular row of seats that swung back and forth like a pendulum. For fifty cents, we could try to make it swing higher and faster by standing up at one of the top seats and heaving our weight back and forth, kind of like pumping a swing. The operator always yelled at us to sit down, but safety was not our chief concern.

"You kids are gonna kill yourselfs," he would say in a heavy Italian accent. "That, or break-a my machine. Either way, it's not good!"

Clearly, he was missing the point. We pushed ever higher and scared the other kids, mostly the girls, half to death. The neighborhood boys and girls, especially the older ones, couldn't get enough.

My friends and I felt like we owned the neighborhood, running the streets with no adult supervision. Certainly, other mothers were there if trouble arose, or if someone got hurt, because we all knew each other. Everyone I knew also had a relative who was in the mafia. I had Uncle Vinny, who was the brother of my uncle on the Bonagura side of the family. (My mother's sister Marietta had married a Bonagura.) Although I didn't know him well, I knew he "took care of things" in our family circle. He was legendary for paying the entire bill for the weddings, funerals, and retirement parties for some friends and family members. And also for refusing to pay for others. I once attended a funeral in Astoria, Queens, for an older cousin who had died of a heroin overdose, and there was concern among those present, while the body lay in the room, about how they were going to pay for the parlor's services.

Someone suggested to "call Vinny." About an hour later, in he walked, a tall Italian man with a big nose and olive complexion. Although it was summer, he was wearing a long wool coat and matching fedora hat. He nodded his head to the room as he walked past the people gathering for the wake and into the manager's office. He closed the door.

About twenty minutes later, the door opened and Uncle Vinny emerged. Without saying a word, he knelt before coffin, said a quick, silent prayer to my cousin's body in the open casket, kissed my grandmother on the cheek and walked out. The next thing we knew, the manager pulled my grandmother aside and whispered that everything had been paid for, including a lunch at a fancy local Italian restaurant the next day that was attended by about fifty people.

Unlike the mafia men in Hollywood movies, Uncle Vinny was a nice guy who often half-kiddingly told his nephews to "stay out of trouble or I'll break your head." Whenever he saw me at a family event or on the street as he drove by in his big black Chrysler, he'd stop and make a point to say hello. It was really an excuse to see what I was up to. He was keeping me in line as a favor to my grandmother, who didn't think my father had it in him to raise me and my siblings properly. It turns out, she was right.

Far from being a gangster, or maybe despite it, Uncle Vinny never allowed us to get involved in illegal things. In those days, to kids my age, that meant breaking into cars. If it had gotten back to Uncle Vinny, I would have received a tongue-lashing from him, and then he would have made me apologize to my mother or grandmother, depending on who was at home when Uncle Vinny hauled me in by the collar of my shirt.

Illegal things may have happened on my block, but nobody ever willingly surrendered information to the cops—or anyone else who asked questions—unless it was absolutely necessary. Houses were broken into; fires were set behind buildings, including one that spread to a nearby deli—we all saw it happen, but nobody said a word. Everyone knew the street code: you keep your mouth shut or you get beaten up. That's what the older kids threatened us with—allegiance or a fat lip. The code worked pretty well. I never ratted on anybody, ever.

***

Life at home was also chaotic. My friends and I would watch as my father came home, staggering in broad daylight, from a night out. Even from two blocks away, we could see him wobbling down the street in a meandering line of drunkenness. He once walked directly into a stop sign and fell to the ground. I had seen him inebriated before, and this time I thought he had safely navigated the sign, but at the last moment he swayed to his left, tried to right himself, and crashed face first into the unforgiving metal pole. I was just a young kid and it took a lot of effort for me to shepherd him inside and up the stairs to our second-floor apartment, but I did, all the while sheepishly hoping that all the neighbors hadn't seen us. When I was teased about it later, I knew they had.

For me, the hard part wasn't my father's fat lip, bloody nose, or puffy face that I helped clean up as a result of his hitting the pole; it was the embarrassment. While none of my friends' dads had a high-paying job, theirs were at least dependable and didn't smell of alcohol most days. Tony Scopello's dad owned a liquor store—and often sold my father booze on credit—yet he didn't behave this way. It made me angry because Cosmo never had a clear explanation of why. Ever. I remember trying to talk to him about it and him brushing me off dismissively.

"Go play on the block," he'd say.

The alcohol had a tight hold over him and wouldn't let go. As a precocious five-year-old, I was stuck with a bum, it was in the open for all to see, and I was ashamed at what my father had become. Even in our rutty neighborhood of Long Island City, his shameless antics were a silent source of mortification.

As Cosmo's drinking escalated, Connie began dating other men and was unfaithful, sometimes "going missing" for two days or more. Grannie often came over to bring food and help pick up the slack. Relatives remember her often covering for her daughter.

"There would be days when no one knew where she was and you would be left alone," said an aunt recounting those days. "Then she would reappear like nothing unusual had happened. Connie played coy but we all knew something was up."

Drunk or sober, Cosmo was abusive to everyone around him, even to us kids for whom he never had much patience. We had a baby grand piano in the foyer of the apartment that my father would play at unpredictable hours of the day and night. When he'd ask me to sit down and try to teach me to play, I, not wanting to have anything to do with him and his drinking, would bang the keyboard with my open hands, which only made him more furious and he'd brush me away.

"Get out of here," he'd admonish. "You don't respect the piano!"

At this point in their marriage, there were many ugly scenes between my parents, which they took turns initiating. My father beat up Connie with his fists and once with a half-empty bottle of whiskey. She, in turn, stabbed him in the hand during one exceptionally bad fight, which he provoked after finding out about another guy she was seeing on the side. It was one of the few times I can remember Connie ever physically standing up to him. She was usually cowering for cover. Rose Ann and I witnessed it all.

I was five, frozen with fear, and couldn't come to my mother's aid. I remember watching, hiding behind my sister and not moving, calloused to the violence after having seen it before.

"What do we do now?" I asked Rose Ann, astounded at what we had just seen. She pulled me close, away from the kitchen where the fight was taking place, sat me down, and held my hand.

"We have to let it happen," she said, taking sides for the first time. "Dad deserves it."

After staring in astonishment at his bleeding hand, my father looked at us and ran from the house. We didn't see him for two days. When he did come back, not a word was spoken about the incident by either my mother or my father. Although I had many questions racing in my head, I didn't ask any of them, and nobody offered any answers. Taking Rose Ann's lead, I learned that it was better to let it go. Like many problems in our small apartment on Ninth Street, the less that was said, the better.

***

Connie was a short, maybe 5'1", and mostly a non-talkative girl growing up. Some called her a "simpleton." Although no formal diagnosis was ever made, there's speculation that she had some type of mental disorder, which would account for her antisocial behavior and failing grades at school. She repeated fifth grade twice. Connie, nonetheless, was regarded as a nice person, always willing to lend a hand when asked. In the few photographs of her that exist, her smile looks forced and uncertain, and in group shots, she's almost always in the background.

She also had a reputation for borrowing money and passing bad checks. The latter got her locked up for six months in the Queens County jail. I have those court records, too.

My grandmother, the stalwart pillar of the family, as much as we had one, stepped in and helped raise us children while Connie was incarcerated. Although Angelina supervised, she didn't live with us, so Charles, who was less than two years old, and I were cared for—fed meager meals, checked to make sure we had two shoes on when we went outside, faces washed, hair combed—by our older sister, Rose Ann.

Even after my mother returned, she and my father stayed out all night—he working and she with the men she was dating—and hardly spoke to each other when they were home. It was clear something had to give. We kids needed adult supervision, but it was Rose Ann that was given the reigns. Not that she asked for it.

It was in the spring of 1966 that Connie was diagnosed with late-stage breast cancer. She had complained about chest pain, but she didn't see a doctor until it was too late. When my mother got sick, she was taken away from us, first to live with my grandmother and later to the hospital, and the life I knew changed drastically. With Connie gravely ill, my grandmother took matters into her own hands and had my mother admitted to a cancer treatment facility without telling my father. Rose Ann and I sat helpless as we watched our mother leave. Cosmo was furious and refused to go to see her. On October 5, 1967, he wrote in his diary:

A girl called and said her name was Cindy and she was a friend of Connie's and that Connie was in the French Hospital and that she had a breast removed and that it was cancer. I told her I wasn't interested and that her mother [Angelina] or sister [Mary] never contacted me.

My father filed a missing person report before he knew where my mother had gone. On October 10th, my father was trying to drop the case:

Called Detective Micca (Missing Persons Bureau) at 3:20. I told her that I knew where my wife was and to drop the case. She wanted me to go to the hospital and peek into the room to make sure that it was my wife. I told her I didn't know she went in or anything and that her mother [Angelina] probably put her in. I also told her I didn't want anything to do with her [Connie] anymore.

She [the detective] was very friendly and told me that she had three kids herself and had hired an Irish woman to take care of them for $50 a week. I told her that was what I wanted to do. She wished me luck and said that I should go to court and get a separation as soon as possible.

That separation plan never panned out and paying a nanny $50 per week was not at all what he planned to do. I was in second grade at St. Rita's Catholic Elementary School in Long Island City when my Uncle Charlie unexpectedly picked me up from school and brought me to his house. He had only done this once before, when my aunt Susie—the oldest of seven Grotticelli siblings—passed away. As I sat in his kitchen, he lit a pipe and the smell of applewood filled the air. His son Angelo once told me he always smoked to ease his nerves. He knew something I didn't.

We were not going home; we were headed to a "new and fun place" for a "little while," so my dad could get us a new place to live. That's what he told us.

"And the best part," said my uncle as we loaded into his car that very evening, "is that it's named after you! Isn't that great? It's called St. Michael's Home."

Even with knowing Cosmo wasn't capable of being a single father, none of his sisters or his brother took us in to live with them. I think he was the black sheep of his family, drinking all of the time, and no one wanted to get involved.

"It's a shame what happened to you kids," said my uncle Willie, years later. But he offered no reason for why they all turned their heads while we were sent away. He, himself, was dumbfounded and seemed to slightly cringe at the very thought. He and his wife, my father's sister Visenza (we called her "aunt Vee"), had adopted a young girl from Italy themselves many years before. But no one on the Grotticelli side stepped in to help us.

However, unbeknownst to me, when Angelina, or Grannie—as every kid on the block called her by then—initially learned we were being sent to St. Michael's, she secretly took us four kids into her apartment (on 30th Ave. and Steinway Street, in Astoria) and literally hid us for a few weeks. She pleaded with the child welfare agency to let us live with her permanently in her small apartment. But my father found out where we were, fought her in court and the New York State Office of Children and Family Services sided with him. They made an "in the best interest of the children" decision that we should be sent to the orphanage because she was also tending to five other grandchildren at the time.

Surely a burden for any woman to handle—no less, one in her mid-60's at the time—she was also mourning the death of her younger daughter Marietta only months earlier. Still, Grannie fought to take us in. She tried everything she could think of to keep us out of the foster care system. No one else in my family ever exhibited courage for my benefit like that.

"We'll find room," she pleaded with the agency, knowing she already had four kids to look after and not daring to let the agent look around too closely. But even now, raising another four in a crowded three-bedroom railroad apartment over a photographer's studio seems implausible to really consider. It was abundantly clear then, too. The child welfare court would not grant her custody, and we Grotticelli kids were shipped off to St. Michael's.

And all this happened by my own father's vindictive design.

"Think of the adventure," my uncle Charles fibbed. If only he had set Cosmo straight. Maybe he should have smacked him around a bit to let Cosmo see that what he was doing was wrong in so many ways.

Who in their right mind gives their kids away? My father, that's who.

***

With lightning speed, and without my mother's know-ledge, three of us were sent to St. Michael's, while my baby sister, Mary, went instead to a private foster home on Long Island. At less than three years old at the time, she was deemed too young for the institutional life.

The orphanage was an imposing series of monolithic brick buildings. The minute I set foot on the grounds, wariness consumed my every breath. For a self-imagined tough kid from Queens, I was nervous and sensed this new reality harbored bad things to come. The place had a bullying air of doom that I had never experienced before. It stank of trouble. I felt this despite the fact that my handlers tried to put me at ease by pointing out innocuous things like "Oh, look at that swing set!" or "They have a slide!" They had dealt with broken families like mine before.

Inside St. Michael's, we were sent to a head nun's office, and Rose Ann, Charles, and I were separated from each other, split by gender and age. We looked at each other but didn't say goodbye. Frozen with fear, we didn't say anything. I just lowered my head was led to a building housing the seven- to ten-year-old boys.

Inside was a large room with dozens of rows of beds, lined up side by side, each with a single clothes locker. About a hundred boys slept there, all subject to unwanted inspections at a moment's notice. Privacy was not even considered. In addition, everything was strictly regimen-ted to keep order. We showered as a group, ate meals together, and settled in for a movie or to listen to records in the evening...together. Individual thinking was not encouraged; you just did what you were told and followed.

I was assigned an empty bed with a small pile of new clothes since, in the rush to take me away from my mother, my father hadn't thought to give me any. I hesitantly sat down and gingerly touched at two changes of clothes and a new pair of black penny-loafers, complete with a shiny penny inserted into the front of each shoe. There was also a small towel, a toothbrush, toothpaste and a bar of soap. At nine, this is what my life had come to.

"This is your new home," said the counselor assigned to me. Then he quickly left. In the stillness by myself, I wondered what was next.

At night, self-tucked in and lying in bed, we'd listen while an old turntable played Walt Disney movie sound-track records or Catholic religion-friendly folk albums that were popular at the time. "The Jungle Book" and the 1965 hit "500 Miles" by the Brothers Four are both ingrained in my memory from that period.

Once established at St. Michael's, I attended P.S. 55, an elementary school on Staten Island. Holding hands with a partner, we lined up each morning to get on the school bus, lined up in the afternoons for the return trip, and lined up again after getting off the bus to walk back to the dorms. I earned good grades and got along with everyone. I liked school; it was a welcome reprieve from the orphanage. In contrast to my interactions at St. Michael's, P.S. 55 was a haven where I was complimented by teachers for my academic diligence and creative interest in music. A fourth-grade report card from this period—dated November 8, 1968—includes a teacher's note that says:

Michael is doing superior work and should be very proud.

He is an enthusiastic reader and successful in all of his work. Hopefully, this will continue next year, as he might enjoy to the fullest his musical talents.

Back at the orphanage, to keep us boys busy (and more importantly, to keep us from fighting with each other), a variety of activities were organized, both officially through the home and unofficially when the supervising nuns weren't looking. One of the unofficial events was Friday Fight Night. This was an event staged by the counselors, who had charge of us after the head nun made her last rounds. The concept was simple: If you had a disagreement with someone, you'd wait until Friday and then box it out (wearing oversized boxing gloves that often slipped off in the middle of a fight) in front of our entire seven-to-ten age group.

It was all kept secret from the nuns and speaking about it meant a certain beating by the counselors. Either way I was going to get punched in the face. Every kid was pushed strongly to pick a fight partner—we weren't called opponents—and we did as we were told. It was seen as an act of bravery to fight and show how tough you were. Like in the streets of Long Island City, it didn't really matter if we got knocked down—and we always did, one way or another—we were judged by how fast we stood back up.

But we had to have a reason to challenge someone, however dubious. I once called a kid into the ring for cutting in front of me that morning in the shower line. I didn't really want to fight this kid, but it was the only excuse I could come up with at the time, and I hadn't fought in a week or two, so I did it. I had to do it or risk being made fun of for being "soft." The counselors kept track of our fight frequency. Unfortunately for me, my partner turned out to be a good fighter and I was left with a bloody nose. I was told to tell the nuns I had fallen in the playground. Ironically, another kid fought someone over a stolen toothbrush and got his tooth knocked out. Such was life in the orphanage.

Whether you agreed with it or not, we all had to live by the sketchy and often-changing rules of Fight Night. The system could be abused and was. A rather large black kid named Michael Washington, age nine, was the most feared person in our dorm. He would challenge a different boy each week to fight him. Just looking at him was excuse enough. I was once forced into our makeshift boxing ring, which was really a square made of corral-style wooden fence partitions and ran away from Michael for the entire time—maybe a few minutes.

His reason for calling me out was that I had, and still have, a nervous habit of uncontrollably, and most times unknowingly, shaking my right leg. Actually, I kept my toe on the floor and hammered my heel up and down many dozen times a minute, depending upon how nervous I was at that moment. That was Michael's excuse and he seized on it.

"I'm gonna knock that shake right outta that leg," he proclaimed loudly, so others could hear.

He certainly gave it his best shot, but—and I still feel proud, decades later—I wasn't beaten up as badly by him as some of the other kids were. He left me with a few bumps and scrapes, but that's it. One kid got a bloody nose and a fat lip for saying Michael's hair looked funny.

One time I got a black eye from a more skilled boy in my group, and the counselors chided me for losing. I had been set up for a pounding. They then coached me to explain to the nuns that I had fallen in the cement yard. Feigning toughness, I wore that injury with honor for a week, knowing that at least it was not at the hands of Michael Washington.

After a few months of this frightening evening event, word got to the nuns and they shut it down. I think a kid's broken jaw gave us away. None of the counselors ever got in trouble, but we kids were collectively punished and had no dessert for a solid week. For an eight-year-old kid, that was a serious consequence.

This was also around the last time I saw Michael Washington. Soon after Fight Night ended, he vanished from our dorm and we were never told why. That happened a lot at St. Michael's. A boy could be there one day and be gone a few weeks or months later without explanation, his empty bed soon filled by another kid.

Other, more officially sanctioned orphanage activities included an Olympics-style track and field competition in the summer months. We were broken up into Red, White, and Blue teams and competed in various athletic events. This orphanage-wide tournament was staged on a wide, well-worn grass field behind the large dormitory buildings where we also played other sports like football and baseball. Our games were always played with a scuffed-up ball, a ripped mitt, and a splintery bat. Nothing was ever new at St. Michael's.

Luckily, I was a fast runner, so I usually won a medal or two in the foot races, which drew the ire of some of my bunkmates.

"You're only fast because you're a little toothpick," said one.

"I could kill you in a fight," instigated another. "Just throw the first punch."

***

To celebrate several of the Catholic holidays, each group of boys and girls put on a concert in a large auditorium for the entire St. Michael's population. On St. Patrick's Day, for example, I was always called upon to be the lead singer in "Michael Row Your Boat Ashore" (my idea), "When Irish Eyes Are Smiling" (not my idea), and "Peg o' My Heart" (then considered a girlie song that none of the boys wanted to sing).

Not every kid appeared in the shows, but along with several other actors and singers, I quickly came to recognize that participating meant rehearsals that kept me away from the dreaded counselors. This, in turn, meant avoiding beatings and bunk chores (another common form of punishment). Even if you weren't that good of a singer—and many were not—you readily signed up and made a fool of yourself onstage. Luckily, I could carry a tune.

My father—who never saw any of my performances, even though he was invited—used to visit us regularly at St. Michael's Home on the first Saturday of every month. However, these highly emotional get-togethers always devolved into sad affairs, with Rose Ann and me pleading with him to take us home. Because my brother Charles was younger, I hardly saw him except on visiting day, so that was another goodbye I had to endure. He typically cried his eyes out each and every time. When these visits were over, we'd wait at the wooden bench next to the

Arthur Kill landfill for the bus to pick up my father and take him away. The stench of the garbage served as a cruel, lingering backdrop.

Once our father was out of sight, Rose Ann, Charles, and I would look at one another despondently without saying much and walk back to our respective dorms, knowing the way without even looking up. Virtually every month it was the same. Our hearts were broken because we wanted to go home. We didn't know it at the time, but we no longer had a home to go back to.

***

Perhaps due to my grandmother and passed on by my mother, religion had always been a big part of my life. Despite their unseemly behavior nearly every day and night during the week, my parents took us to church on most Sundays and raised us in the Roman Catholic faith. Or at least our convenient version of it. Connie and Cosmo themselves weren't the godly type and probably would not have seen the inside of a church as often as they did if not for my grannie. She was deeply religious, if a bit uneducated, and liked to take matters into her own hands. If Grannie said we had to go to church, we all went. Growing up in Long Island City in the 1960s, you had no choice but to be a practicing Catholic—even if you weren't really "practicing" as Jesus had intended, so my grandmother made sure we went to church.

Angelina was naturally funny when she didn't mean to be. She constantly lectured us with her homemade reasoning, which routinely came out sounding comical. She mixed up clichés, saying things like "He smokes like a fish," "He drinks like a chimney," or "That's the worst smell I ever heard." But we knew what she meant.

Because of my religious upbringing, shortly after arriving at the orphanage I volunteered to be an altar boy during Sunday Mass at St. Michael's. There was a small church right on campus. It wasn't a conscious religious decision, but more of a gravitational pull toward something I didn't really understand but knew instinctively was the right thing for me to do. Due to my uneven Roman Catholic upbringing, I had always liked the way the altar boys looked in their black-and-white robes as they helped the priests serve "the body of Christ"—a thin, chalky-tasting wafer—to the congregants. Altar boys even got to ring a bell on cue when the priest raised the chalice containing "God's blood"—wine—over his head. That was a big thing for a seven-year-old.

Up on the altar, I was initially overcome with nerves, thinking that everyone was staring at me. I often got the timing wrong and rang the bell before the priest had finished speaking. However, after a few stern looks from Father Kenny, the head priest, and a bit of practice, I became one of the best altar boys at hosting Mass and was asked to serve more than some of the others. I felt a sense of power on the altar, and more importantly, Father Kenny said I was "saving the world."

He was a graying, soft-spoken man who was well liked by all of the kids at St. Michael's. We looked forward to his regular dorm visits when he would gather us boys in a circle and we would be transfixed by the funny and sometimes scary stories he told. They didn't come from a book; they were all in his mind.

"Now don't tell the nuns about that," he'd say half-jokingly after realizing we were wide-eyed and trembling. Then he'd tell another story, and we'd gratefully hang on his every word.

***

Terminally ill and agonizing over the fact that her children had been taken away, my mother died alone in a hospital bed on Father's Day, June 18, 1968. She was forty-one years old. My grandmother said that dying on Father's Day was Connie's final revenge against Cosmo. I hoped she was right.

I had only visited her in the hospital once during my stay at St. Michael's, in May of that year, and I brought her a small orange marigold in a flower pot I got from school to cheer her up.

The day after my mother's death, Father Kenny called me to his office in the rectory, and I immediately noticed he was holding the flower pot. The single marigold was droopy from a lack of water, and he handed it to me abruptly.

"God needed her to serve him," he said, trying to console me. All of eight years old, I was livid that God could be so selfish.

"How could he need her more than I do?" I said. It wasn't right.

He struggled to find words, looking down and tentative.

"Sometimes we don't understand God's will but must simply obey it," he said. It was the voice of the church speaking. "We've all been welcomed to assist the Catholic Church. Your mother lived a good Christian life. Now it's her time to serve. That should be enough for you."

My inability to comprehend his reasoning shook my religious belief to the core, and that feeling has stuck with me my entire life. I was done with being an altar boy. As much as I tried to understand what the priest was saying, I couldn't grasp the reality of it. I had seen her smiling a month before, and she had asked if I was happy. I lied and said, "Yes."

For weeks after she died, I would lie awake at night thinking of what cancer had taken from me. I also wondered if it was going to kill me too. It seemed like literally everything was being taken from me and I was powerless to stop it. What theft would tomorrow bring?

All I could do was hope hard for something better. I had no idea exactly what I was hoping for or where it would come from, but I knew that somehow, some way, I needed to—and would—get out of that dreadful situation.

Ever the optimist, I urgently wanted the Grotticellis to be a family again, as much as the mental image I'd conjured up in my young mind knew what that meant. I prayed, as all altar boys are taught to do, with increasing regularity, asking for better things to come. I craved a home life for my sisters and brother, and even for my father. I was after a loving and supportive whole. According to the nuns, without my mother, God would show me the way. However, in my eyes, God had taken my mother when I needed her most, and I couldn't get that anger out of my head.

As for the beating I took in the bathroom for refusing to give up my Holy Communion ring, the lashing stopped once it started to leave a noticeable, lasting mark. The counselors realized that I wasn't giving it up. Not this time.

That ring was all I had, really, a critical part of me, like a right arm, that I'd rather die than relinquish. With my mother gone, my family in ruins, my other worldly possessions mysteriously missing and my spirit sorely tested, it meant so much more than a piece of jewelry. It was my soul that was in danger.

Later that night, I lay awake on my stomach to avoid irritating my back wounds, clutching that small gold-and-garnet ornament in my quivering little hand. Even with my dissatisfaction with the church, I prayed for something better in my life...and vowed never to let that ring go.

<u>2</u>

MY SHIP CAME IN

After almost two and a half years of keeping my fingers (and toes) crossed tightly for luck, my prayers were finally answered, and my long nightmare at St. Michael's came to an end in the summer of 1969. The outside world was positively aligning that year. My favorite football team, the New York Jets, had won the NFL championship game, beating the Baltimore Colts in Super Bowl III. And my baseball team, the New York Mets, were in an improbable pennant race that eventually lead to a World Series title. And on Sunday, August 3rd, 1969, I got word that I was being sent to live with a "nice family in the country."

Shock. Astonishment. Joy. None of those words adequately describe my elation. This was freedom in the best way I could imagine—and the biggest exhalation of relief I'd ever had.

My enthusiasm soon got the better of me and I began giving my few possessions—a baseball glove and some comic books—to the boy who slept next to me in the dormitory.

"I'm not giving them back," said my incredulous bunkmate.

I'd been on the receiving end before, so I understood his negotiation position. There was always the chance I'd be coming back. And at St. Michael's, the rule among delinquents was: "If I'm holding it in my hand, it's mine."

My head counselor told me that morning I would be going to Long Island, New York, to stay with a family called the Nelsons. I didn't have a choice, of course, and I wasn't being picky. Names meant nothing, joining a new family was the prize I was after, and it looked like I had won.

Yes, it was finally a reality. Like a prisoner who had done his time, I was getting out! A huge weight lifted from my shoulders. The Nelsons sounded respectable, especially since there had been a famous television show called *The Adventures of Ozzie and Harriet*, starring Ozzie and Harriet Nelson and their two sons. We watched the reruns in a lounge area of the orphanage.

To that point, I'd been born into a poor Italian family and shipped off to an abusive orphanage—neither of which I chose. I wanted the Nelson life.

***

I spoke with a social worker from the Angel Guardian Agency, the organization in charge of my life, who told me that the Nelsons were a foster family. I had never heard that term before. I asked the counselor if foster care was a real family. One where you were loved and could love back. One that you woke up to every day and went to sleep with every night. Where the parents took the time to be with you and do things together. I never had that. Maybe, just maybe—because nothing was certain—I was getting that now.

"We'll see how it works out, but I have a good feeling about this," he said, working from the same script he used on all of his charges. "It's going to be fun."

That might have been standard hyperbole, but he and I both knew I was one of the lucky ones. I was worried that I would be going without my sisters and brother. Were they coming too? I didn't want to be separated from them again. Then I got a phone call from my father, telling me Rose Ann and Charles were indeed going with me. Phone calls from my father were scarce, and this was the rarest of good news.

The agency had deemed the Nelsons' home as "the ideal situation" for us, as they were known among the child placement agents for taking in multiple kids at a time from a single family. I was thrilled and started asking him questions about how we'd get there.

"You're going to a new place," my father told me over the phone, knowing how much I hated being at St. Michael's Home and trying to sound as if he were responsible for giving us a better life. That's all he said; he didn't even mention my other sister, Mary Theresa. I found out later that she would not be joining us at the Nelsons. She was too young for St. Michael's, so another foster family adopted her while we were in the orphanage.

This news left me feeling a bit empty inside and it collided internally with the good news. I wanted Mary to live with us as well.

"How soon?" I asked, not able to contain my excitement. "Can we go *now*?"

"These things take time," my father said, being deliberately vague because he had no control.

After a brief silence on the phone, he said, "You should be happy."

"I am," I said, "but will you be there?"

"No," he answered. "You'll be better off there without me."

That last sentence should have cut like a knife. I had already experienced a life with little supervision, or love really, from him. But nothing could damper my enthuse-iasm for leaving St. Michael's. Leaving couldn't happen soon enough.

The paperwork took another two long days. So, I impatiently waited, my leg shaking instinctively, from Sunday until Tuesday, when my personal liberation finally came. Since I had given away all my stuff, my life's possessions now amounted to two changes of clothes and a worn pair of penny-loafers. And, of course, my Holy Communion ring, worn religiously on my right-hand ring finger.

I woke up earlier than usual that day, hours before many of the other kids, got dressed, and ran to the head nun's office to get my official release papers. The security guards on my floor didn't try to stop me, waving good-bye in an uninterested way. Everybody knew I was being released. The other kids were jealous but happy for me. Having personally seen worse done to other kids, I was leaving relatively unscathed. It was almost hard to fathom that I was really and truly getting out. Regardless of the years of industrial mistreatment, my parting mood was not animosity. I think for the first time ever, I felt joy.

So, my siblings and I left that dark chapter at St. Michael's behind us, excited yet emotionally spent. Rose Ann, Charles, and I came into the Nelsons' home clinging to a hope for something that would bring stability to our lives.

Stability—that was my definition of family—here I come!

3

NINA HAD A DREAM

Who could have guessed that a blunt, stubborn, no-nonsense, deeply religious, battle-axe of a woman from the other side of Queens would be my savior?

She was born Filomena "Nina" Marie Alifano on February 15, 1923. Relatives say she was a bright but pigheaded kid, the second of four children in the Alifano family. Often referred to as "a little Hitler" by her friends, Nina earned straight A's at P.S. 20 and later at Flushing High School, but never officially graduated. Set to be valedictorian of her class in 1941, she had a dispute with her English teacher regarding an assignment she refused to complete. Faced with the choice of finishing the paper or not graduating, the characteristically stubborn Nina chose the latter and walked away without a diploma.

Years later, she still held firm to the conviction that she had made the right decision. That's the kind of ego she had.

After two years of working odd jobs, Nina secretly joined the WAVES (Women Accepted for Volunteer Emergency Service), a unit of the U.S. Naval Reserve during World War II. The nation was in a state of fear of the Germans taking over the world at that time, so thousands of young women were signing up to join the fight. Domineering citizens like Nina were a welcome stateside support system for the troops fighting overseas.

For her personally, it was a chance to get out of her parents' house and look important in the eyes of those around her. Everyone said Nina craved attention.

When her mother and father, Mary Pauline (Fino) and Vincent Alifano, found out their daughter had enlisted, they were furious, even threatened to disown her, but could not dissuade her. Nina soon left for the Mare Island Naval Shipyard in Vallejo, California, where she held several secretarial jobs. The naval base was 3,000 miles from where she had grown up and farther from home than any Alifano had ever traveled.

After rising to the rank of petty officer first class, Nina was discharged in the spring of 1944. She came home, and her sisters, Rosamunda and Marie, helped her get a job as a keypunch operator for the American Insurance Company in New York City. Nina's future sister-in-law Arline, who later married Nina's younger brother Vitale (aka "Sonny") worked there as well. They quickly all got along fine, even away from work. Nina moved up the ladder rapidly and within a year was supervising a group of female keypunch operators.

By 1945, Nina was set to marry a man named Danny, who was a few years younger than she was. However, two weeks before the wedding, Nina and her mother were shopping for a new dress when she surprised her mother with the news that she had met someone else. This new gentleman, Gilbert Joseph Nelson, was studying electrical engineering and lived in Brooklyn with his parents, Julia and David. The young suitor also had an older brother named Walter, who lived in Texas. Unbeknownst to Nina's father, both David and Walter were infamous in their family for their aloofness and drinking problems. This was the early sixties, and character flaws like this were swept under the rug.

Gilbert, she was sure, didn't have any of those bad qualities.

He joined the Air Force in 1942 as an instrument specialist and eventually rose to the rank of corporal. After leaving the service in 1945, he later worked at IBM as a field technician. This new job caused him to make regular visits to the American Insurance Company offices to fix the keypunch card machines.

He met Nina in 1945 after being sent to fix her machine. They married five years later, on June 10, 1950, and settled into an apartment in Brooklyn. It was a meager one-bedroom place, but no one they knew had anything bigger in those days.

"I thought he was silly," she told me years later, explaining what attracted her to Mr. Nelson. "And he liked to dance. Most boys back then didn't like to dance, but he could cut a rug like no one I knew."

It turns out he was a better-than-average dancer. Thanks to Gilbert's agile moves learned in the local dance halls as a kid, he walked into the Arthur Murray School in Brooklyn one day and became an instructor within two weeks, teaching regularly at night to make extra money.

***

Looking for more space, Nina and Gilbert moved with other family members to a small house in College Point, Queens owned by her father. Nina was a dedicated career woman. After she gave birth to their first son, Gilbert J. Nelson, Junior, on May 16, 1951, she went back to work within a few weeks and left her mother to care for the new baby.

After two years, the couple tired of city life and decided to move to the country, which meant anywhere outside of the city. They decided to look on Long Island. At the time, sprawling farms that produced dairy products, corn and potatoes still dominated the landscape out east. Property was relatively cheap, as long as you didn't mind building a house on a dirt field. Suburban neighborhoods were only starting to be developed. So, looking for their piece of the American dream, and with his head filled with ideas, Gilbert decided to design and build the house himself on a 27,000-square-foot lot (.62 acres) in the Suffolk County town of Huntington.

While most neighboring homes cost roughly $18,000 to build, the budget for the Nelsons' rose well above $35,000. On the outside, the house included rough-hewn cedar shingles, a hand-cut sandstone fireplace, and a large two-bay garage. Inside, were four bedrooms, a floor-to-ceiling sandstone fireplace, a grand eight-foot-wide stair-case in the foyer that majestically ascended to the second floor with triangle-shaped sandstone planters on either side, a living room with a twelve-foot ceiling, exposed dark wood beams, and dark wood paneling on the walls, a moderate dining room, and a large kitchen. The plan was a spilt-level design with a lower level in the rear of the house and a large basement with a metal cellar storm door that opened to the outside.

The young Nelsons enlisted the entire Alifano family to bring the impressive plan to fruition. Family members were strongly—Nina's brother, Al, would say—enlisted to help with the construction. They didn't really want to do the work and politely tried to say so in different ways. Yet, they all pitched in to build Gilbert's dream. Nina was that persuasive.

After four years of toiling in the dirt, Al and his new wife, Arline, decided they'd had enough of working on the Huntington house every weekend. The often-over-whelming workload became a recurring cause of angst within the entire Alifano family. With some prodding from Arline, who halfheartedly threatened to leave him if they spent another weekend working on "someone else's house," Al told Nina they needed a break. She refused to talk to him for several months. She did this more than once, and then, just as suddenly, she would call and reestablish the relationship. It was always on her terms. Thus, due to the sheer will of Nina and Gilbert, the house was progressing, albeit at a slow pace, and—family be damned—the Nelsons continued doing most of the work themselves.

In 1958, with the bulk of the structural beams in place but the interior walls and floors still unfinished, the Nelsons left their cramped life in College Point behind for good. Along with Gil Jr. and a new baby boy, Gerard Michael, who was born on September 23, 1957, they moved into 12 Bryant Drive in Huntington. Mrs. Nelson soon quit her job in order to focus on being a full-time mother to her two young boys.

Within several months, progress on the house slowed down as the construction drained the family's financial and physical resources. Then an unexpected solution revealed itself to Mrs. Nelson as a way to help make ends meet. Her sister Rose had brought a foster child named Emily into her home in Smithtown, and then another named Lucille. Mrs. Nelson learned that Rose was getting paid by the state of New York to care for these girls. It was Peter Brenna, Rose's husband, who originally came up with the foster care idea.

A light bulb went on in Nina's head. Mr. Nelson remained mostly silent when they first discussed the idea. He wanted a typical American family and raising other people's kids wasn't his way of doing it. However, as always when they disagreed, Mrs. Nelson won the argument and got what she fancied. Setting a precedent that would continue for the rest of their lives together, Mr. Nelson was not a fighter. Without any lengthy discussion, he gave in.

"I'll make a few phone calls," Nina said.

The Nelsons accepted a fifteen-year-old boy named Andrew J. Fawcett into their home in June of 1960. Andy came from the Angel Guardian Child Welfare Agency of New York. Soon there was another foster child, a girl named Diane, who had been unofficially transferred from Mrs. Nelson's sister, Rose. The agency allowed it without objection. This was done "between sisters" so as not to attract attention to the physical abuse occurring at the Brenna house.

Many people in both families knew about the abuse. The evidence—bruises and broken legs suffered by Diane and a broken arm inflicted on her foster sibling Lucille— was indisputable, yet no one openly discussed it. The Brenna kids were getting hurt, and the Angel Guardian Agency didn't see anything amiss.

Not satisfied with four children—two natural and two foster—Mrs. Nelson next brought a six-year-old named Steven ("little Stevie") into the large but still unfinished Huntington house. Then, a few months later, a fourteen-year-old boy named John arrived.

But there were limits to her patience, and she was clearly not interested in problem children. Both Steven and John were sent back to the agency within a few months of arriving. John for allegedly stealing from the Nelsons, and Stevie for being excessively hyperactive and repeatedly jumping off the couch and landing head-first onto the floor.

"Shape up or ship out!" she liked to say.

Over the next five years, new groups of kids from three different families came to stay. First Kim and Darren Newfield; then Melody and Glenn Keppler; and finally Rose Ann, Charles, and I. As an agency document stated, the Nelsons became known at the agency as "a positive and unique repository for groups of more than one child." The goal for everyone involved in foster care is always to keep siblings together whenever possible, but most foster families won't take more than one child.

So, after several single-child experiments, the Nelsons began accepting two or three related children at a time, and the foster care money came rolling in.

Counting Andy, there were now eight foreigners in Gil Jr.'s and Gerry's young lives. We were a bunch of disdained, unwanted urchins usurping their parents' attention and their home.

However, Mrs. Nelson was not about to change things. This foster parent scheme killed two birds with one stone: it helped pay the bills and it fulfilled her dream of having a large family. By 1977, the Nelsons received $218 for each child, which worked out to about $1,744 per month. Mrs. Nelson was now bringing in nearly as much as Mr. Nelson earned as at IBM.

In addition, Mrs. Nelson appeared heroic and altruistic for "saving these kids from the streets," as she liked to tell anyone who would listen. How she looked to the outside world—maintaining that center of attention—was paramount to her. Mrs. Nelson always craved positive attention, even as a child roaming the streets of Flushing. Al said she felt she was better—more decent, more religious—than everyone around her.

Mrs. Nelson's fantasy of a troop of kids who would assemble obediently on command like the Von Trapp children did in *The Sound Of Music* when their father whistles was alive and well. From my point of view, and for the other foster kids making up this newly expanded Nelson family, it was an exciting time, full of unknown possibilities and thrilling aspirations.

4

A TEPID WELCOME HOME

The 90-minute drive to the Nelson house in Huntington was both nerve-racking and interminable. A million thoughts raced through my head. Would there be bars on the windows like there were at St. Michael's? Would I always have to watch my back? The voice in my head screamed with anxiety, yet Rose Ann and Charles didn't speak for the entire car ride. The three of us were bunched together in the back seat, Charles in the middle. I tried relentlessly to get Rose Ann, whom I hadn't seen in a week, to say something. Anything.

"Isn't there anything you want to say?" I asked, hoping to break the dread of the unknown the situation presented. She just stared out the window.

Charles was teary-eyed and mostly sobbed, his pain on

display for all to see though I couldn't figure out what he was crying about. The right-side sleeve of my shirt was soaked from his wiping. He gave short, one-word responses to my questions, like "Yes" and "I don't know" and "No," without even thinking first. Feeling alone in my apprehension about what lie ahead, I consoled myself with the hope that wherever we were going was be better than where we had been.

And it was.

For me, a kid from the raw streets of Queens and then from the harsh orphanage, Huntington was the most open, rural, and green place I had ever seen. This was better than a movie, more vibrant than a painting and instantly calming. I was intoxicated with the newness of it all. My new life rushed over me in exhilarating waves of fascinating smells and physical things I had never been so close to—like a giant Mulberry tree or a pond with catfish. The sun shone bright that day, brighter than I had ever seen it, and the feeling was pure exuberance. It was freedom from all I had feared for the past two years and a look into a future I dreamed about and prayed hard for.

Large and small sweet-smelling trees and plants were everywhere, complemented by large areas of the greenest grass and crisp cloud-filled blue skies. Gone was the garbage stench. It was verdant and literally breathtaking. I began singing to myself, that's how unbridled my happiness was. The house was big to my nine-year-old eyes, and much cozier than the monolithic buildings I had grown used to. That made it immediately welcoming.

Mrs. Nelson was waiting at the front door. When I first saw her standing there with her hands on her hips, I immediately sensed that she was a no-nonsense kind of woman. At forty-six, Mrs. Nelson carried a little extra weight on her medium size frame. She was slightly taller than my five foot six inches, with shoulder-length, silver-white hair framing her makeup-free, round face. The plain shirt and pants she wore were somewhat unkempt, as if she had just finished cleaning the entire house and was taking a much-needed break.

She ventured a cordial smile, which seemed to mask a familiar curiosity of what they were getting this time. Her eyes conveyed a suspicion of who we were and what kind of trouble we would cause. It must have been that way with all the kids when they first arrived. She was sizing us up.

We stood in the doorway for a few seconds exchanging pleasantries, but instead of welcoming us inside the house, Mrs. Nelson led us to an aluminum patio table in the backyard.

"It's better if you wait outside," she said, catching us a bit off guard after a long emotional car ride. She physically blocked us from going inside her home.

"Why don't you go sit in the backyard until the other kids get here."

Other kids? The agency counselor had told us about this "nice big family" we would be calling our own, and it was now almost a reality. I was excited at the prospect of making new friends but terrified of having to watch my back against what they might do, or who I would have to fight. I was feeling hope and fear tightly wound together.

Mrs. Nelson spoke privately to the counselor who had brought us for about thirty minutes while we three waited in the backyard, bewildered and not saying much to one another. When the adults were finished, the counselor left, making our transition from wards of the state to wards of the Nelsons complete, although not officially sealed. Mrs. Nelson still had the choice to give us back if things didn't work out.

I sat with my hyperactive leg moving a mile a minute.

"Are you nervous?" she said, pointing out my jackhammering leg. "I gotta work on that."

Freedom felt good, but it also made me anxious. I made sure to keep my insecurities to myself, as I had learned to do at the orphanage. *Keep your head down.*

After some small talk, I carefully found the courage to tell Mrs. Nelson I was hungry. I was avoiding getting under her skin so quickly. She went into the house and returned with plain, unflavored yogurt. I had never eaten yogurt and hated the slimy texture and the bitter taste. I didn't want to sound ungrateful, but it was awful in so many ways. Taking the upper hand from the start, Mrs. Nelson delicately yet defiantly said I had to finish that yogurt or I could not get up from the table.

While Rose Ann and Charles ate their portions in a few minutes, I held out for about two hours. Mrs. Nelson was not letting me leave that table until I had eaten every last spoonful. Finally, I closed my eyes and swallowed hard. Nothing could ruin the euphoria of that day.

With the yogurt gone, we sat there on that warm August afternoon for about an hour more, waiting for "the other kids" to come home. The anticipation fueled my leg to continue its nonstop pace. We talked with Mrs. Nelson for a while longer about trivial things like the weather and the car ride over.

Without our knowledge, Mr. Nelson had deliberately drove past the house to see if we had arrived. They were as anxious to see us as we were them. Mr. Nelson turned the family's late-1950s blue Mercury station wagon into the driveway and Kim, Melody, Glenn, and Darren came out back to say hello. We greeted each other sheepishly, but to my relief got along right away. They immediately understood who I was and why I was here. We made small talk and Glenn asked if I liked sports.

"The New York Mets are the best," I said.

"I don't like sports," he offered.

"That's because he runs like a wacky turtle," Melody said.

An immediate and emotionally natural connection was formed. Gil Jr. and Gerry, however, were not there to meet us.

Once we settled in, life became as happy as it had ever been for Rose Ann, Charles, and me. To truly understand the dynamics of this particular group of foster kids, you have to picture eight people as different in looks as there could be. Our features and mannerisms were as distinctive and different as *The Village People*. Melody was assertive but friendly. Kim was ditzy and kept mixing up words when she spoke. Glenn was shy and had a weak handshake. And Darren, the smallest of the group, stared at the floor a lot and didn't say anything. We all shook hands and followed Mr. Nelson into the house.

We had come from four separate dysfunctional backgrounds, but we immediately felt like kin, as they say in the South, as fast as you could say "family."

***

While befriending the other kids felt natural to me

personally, we Grotticellis inexplicably began to avoid each other. I was a chatterbox but Rose Ann chose to hide in the background and never volunteered an opinion on anything. She seemed content to simply agree with whatever was being discussed, whether she actually did or not. She wasn't acting normal and I was cut out of her new existence.

"I don't want to talk about it," was her common response to any conversation. She was sealing herself into her shell, even from me. That was very unlike her. We always spoke about things, there was a time when we two were all we had. Now we had nothing to say to each other.

She was short (five feet, two inches) with brown hair, a nervous smile that rarely showed teeth, a slim medium build, and a bad habit of wringing her hands together like a mad scientist while she was thinking. The later usually happened at the most inappropriate times. I often told her she was pretty just to boost her spirits and remove that sad expression from her face. Our early experiences with our parents in Queens had taken a huge toll on her personally and affected how she interacted with other people. Now, I was bearing the brunt of her anti-social behavior, with the two of us visibly growing apart.

Thankfully, she had now stopped talking to herself like she did when we were younger, but she was also highly sensitive to criticism and when she got mad, she wouldn't speak to me for days. She sheepishly mingled with the other kids, especially the girls, and didn't associate much with Gil Jr. and Gerry. She was also very wary of Mrs. Nelson and was never comfortable calling her "mom."

Charles ("Charlie") was also small in size (Grotticelli genes) and extremely unassuming. He had a large welcoming smile with big teeth that dominated his smile—that is, when he wasn't crying or pouting about something. He was always scared and unsure of what to say or do when the Nelsons were around, often looking down at the floor to avoid eye contact. Sometimes he'd hang onto my shirt tail. It was his way of coping. Mrs. Nelson tried to encourage him to get involved with the other kids, but he resisted and so she left him to acclimate on his own. Charles was more of a project for her, and she didn't have the patience she'd once had back when Andy was young.

Charles rarely offered the first, or last, word. He was a kid who craved attention, but instead, stayed quiet to avoid saying the wrong thing. Offending anyone was probably his biggest fear. When you got him going, though, he was a "kidder," telling jokes that weren't really funny, but the way he told them made you laugh heartily, nonetheless. And he nervously laughed at his own jokes.

He was quick to volunteer when we'd put on family variety shows. Charles also excelled in the school band as a trombone player, perhaps owing to our father's musical background.

There's no doubt that after being released from the orphanage, and once I became comfortable with my Nelson surroundings, there weren't enough hours in the day to take it all in. I was enthusiastically interested in everything. Back then, I was as scared as anyone but became really good at hiding it, eventually leading the pack in terms of always being the one to come up with something for us to do to pass the time.

I'd make guitars out of cardboard and pieces of wood and a drum set out of overturned five-gallon cans. Then

I'd play Beatles records and we would mime the words and pretend-play our instruments.

"This is stupid," Glenn would say.

"I hate the drums," Darren would echo.

"My guitar looks terrible," said Charles.

It was a valiant effort on my part. There were many times when we were left to our own devices once our chores were done, and I saw my job as keeping us out of sight for more chores. I also organized the games we played outside (like "war" with sticks as guns and mud balls as bombs) and inside (usually board games like one I made up called "getaway," where we moved a game piece around a board, committing various crimes and "running" from the police). I also asked a million questions of my teachers at school and of the Nelsons, who both admitted to me that I got annoying at times.

"Keep it down," I was told a lot, by both Mr. and Mrs. Nelson.

"Don't ask so many questions," Mrs. Nelson would say. "Go get a book from the library. Do not use the Time-Life set at home. That's for school reports."

We had an aging set of The Encyclopedia Britannica that was fair game to use but not those new Time-Life books, with their colorful photographs and each copy dedicated to a different subject, like "Sharks" or Plants." They were "expensive" she said, having recently purchased them from a traveling salesman, while the encyclopedia set was several years old. We weren't allowed to touch those new reference books unless we had a special school assignment due. This rule was strictly enforced, although I secretly looked at them on other occasions, making sure no one saw me.

"Don't be rough with those books, we have to save them for everybody to use," Mrs. Nelson said, often, looking over our backs as we perused the pages.

"I'm trying to expand my knowledge," I'd say, although that wasn't always true. Sometimes I just liked to look at the lifelike pictures that could mentally take you to another exotic place.

"Yeah right, and if I believe that, you'll be trying to sell me quicksand to build a house on," was her snarky response.

Being an avid reader of kid's books, I did have one book that I referred to often. Due to my hyper-inquisitiveness, my fourth-grade teacher gave me a book at Christmas called *Answers and More Answers*, which featured factual scientific explanations in response to common questions like "Why do humans yawn?" and "How does a sneeze work?" The nerd in me always wanted to know these inane things...and still does.

***

This amusingly unconventional collection of housemates were now "my people." And although it would take a while to learn their specific likes and dislikes, each had experienced surprisingly similar hardships in their lives, so we instinctively related. Although we never spoke about them to anyone, or even to each other, the communal feelings of loss and longing for parents helped secure an immediate and close alliance among us: one that Gil Jr. and Gerry didn't share. In their minds it was us against them.

I only learned the other foster kids' backstories much

later in life, but after hearing them, my own perspective changed. I realized didn't have a monopoly on misery. We were destined to get along.

5

ADOPTION ON A STRING

Ever since we arrived at the Nelsons' home, the thought of belonging to this family had grown from an aspiration to motivation. About a year after we came to the house, Mrs. Nelson surprised Charles and I with the idea that she was interested in adopting us. For a foster kid, this is like getting released into a toy store with no spending limits.

I was puzzled at first. Adoption had been a dream of almost everyone's at St. Michael's, but the word scared me, and apparently Mr. Nelson as well. I secretly heard him and Mrs. Nelson arguing about the cost. So, I looked it up in the Encyclopedia Britannica set in the house in secrecy, avoiding Mrs. Nelson's cherished Time-Life books. I was researching a promise made.

It said: *Adoption, the act of establishing a person as*

parent to one who is not in fact or in law his or her child.

So that's how a parent was gotten, I concluded, if you didn't already have one. I just had to establish someone. In my mind, I had settled on the Nelsons as my parents. It felt good saying the word out loud.

As it turned out, all the other foster kids had been promised adoption as well, so the idea was sounding better and better. I needed a mother and father, desperately, and we were all doing it together. That's all the motivation I needed. My biological father had to agree to the adoption, but there was no resistance from him. On May 23rd 1975, after eight years of living with the Nelsons, Cosmo (whom we had taken to calling "other father" at this point) agreed to sign papers relinquishing his parental rights forever during a preliminary adoption hearing.

During the proceeding, and on a break from college, Rose Ann testified before the court that she "approved" of us all being adopted and paved the way for Charles and me. She herself was not interested and never warmed to the idea of a new mother. Yet, for Cosmo, letting us go meant scribbling his signature on an unsympathetic piece of paper. It should not have been so easy.

So, even if Rose Ann didn't want a new parent, I did. Andy had been adopted by the Nelsons, and I was eager to be part of the club.

Once the hearing was over, I was officially known as a "neglected child" and "legally freed for re-parenting" per a judge's ruling on June 23rd, and a piece of paper that still sits in the King's County Clerk's office in Brooklyn.

My sister, Mary, initially lived with another foster family as an infant while we were in St. Michael's, but was transferred to the Nochese family about a year after we arrived in Huntington. However, the Angel Guardian Agency would not allow Mary to join us at the Nelsons.

As a result, John and Marie Nochese, of Brentwood, officially adopted Mary when she was ten years old. She grew up there with the Nocheses' natural sons John, Jr., and Michael, as well as another adopted daughter, Annabelle, and was happy. We saw Mary regularly during visits with my father on the first Sunday of every month at the Angel Guardian offices in Mineola, New York. Those visits were always highly anticipated and then over in a flash, only to be repeated each month.

Unfortunately, time went by and our adoption never happened. The promise wasn't kept. I wondered if Mr. Nelson had won the argument, which was rare for him. Perhaps it was because it cost money to file the paperwork, more money than the Nelsons were willing to spend. Their true reason for not going through with it, however, was different than what they told the agency. In a document dated May 25, 1975, a caseworker wrote:

Foster parents are interested in adopting Michael and Charles. However, they are concerned about adopting at this time because of the adverse effects this might have on another foster child in their home they are not adopting at this time because of this child's emotional problems. This child wishes adoption and may feel rejected and act out. The parents are concerned as this child is fifteen years old and has been in the home for twelve years and they feel she is a full part of the family. They have hesitated to take full responsibility through adoption of this child due to her emotional and behavioral problems, and her need for on-going treatment.

Like me, Kim, Melody and Glenn were all fifteen years old at the time, so it's not clear who "another foster child" mentioned in this report refers to. It was probably Melody, as each time she came back from the forced trips to see her mother in Florida, she was unruly and sent to a psychiatrist who gave her medication (Ritalin) to calm her "anger issues," in the words of an agency doctor. It was clear that for Melody, staying with her natural mother was not healthy, so Mrs. Nelson tried to limit the visits. When Melody was back home, she was her old bossy self, and we all felt better for it.

For Mrs. Nelson, having us all at home and not visiting our natural parents was preferred. She used the carrot of adoption to keep us on our best behavior and keep the world thinking the Nelsons' home was a successful and nurturing place. In reality it was both good and bad, depending upon Mrs. Nelson's mood. That made her frustrating to gauge. The good days made the bad ones tolerable. Adoption made foster care a bit more palatable.

By now growing up in the Nelson house was a regimented existence and, to me, felt more and more like my former stay in the orphanage. Individuality and opinion were not welcome. The days were filled with school, Sunday mornings at church, mandatory chores on weekdays, exact dinner times that were not to be missed, and "busy work" (chores to take up time and keep us occupied) on weekends. There was no opportunity for outside friends.

That's why keeping up appearances meant so much: the payments from the state for each foster kid would continue to arrive. For us, it meant another aspiration dashed. We'd have to live with the "foster child" moniker, whether we liked it or not. Long story short: despite the genuine-sounding assurances to us all, Andy was the only foster kid the Nelsons ever adopted, and today, he wishes he wasn't.

For a brief moment the finish line of family permanence was within sight but, regrettably, it was never reached.

6

BROTHERS UNDER SIEGE

For Gilbert Jr. and Gerry Nelson, this pseudo-philan-thropic lifestyle of taking in other people's kids was an unwelcome disruption: from the first foster kid, Andy, to the last, me.

Their once stable home had become unhinged; a place where they didn't know whether or when a new kid would arrive at the front door. These new kids had a habit of showing up without warning. They just came, and left, and came back again, and came, and came. And most didn't leave. To Gil Jr. and Gerry, the worst part was that they were never consulted beforehand. This was clearly not *their* idea. Gil Jr. felt he was being pushed aside as this endless stream of strangers relegated him further and further—physically and emotionally—from his parents, and it had a lasting effect. His father was spending more time with these new kids than he did with Gil Jr., and that didn't feel good.

According to relatives, Mrs. Nelson spoke to Gil Jr. when he was about twelve years old about her idea of "saving" the children. This was after the first two or three foster kids had already come and gone. Gil Jr. told her he was wholeheartedly against it, but Mrs. Nelson didn't pay attention to his protests and rarely spoke about the matter with him again. There was no negotiation about these actions that would change his life forever.

The constant influx caused Gil Jr. to retreat into himself and, later, a small circle of undesirable friends. It was upsetting for him to see that not only was he now not the only child in the house, he wasn't even the oldest. He wanted nothing to do with our band of gypsies and growing up, he usually avoided all contact. Well, at least with us boys. Gil Jr. had a wandering eye for Kim and Melody, and probably any female at that time, and sexually propositioned them on a few occasions when the girls were around fourteen. He didn't push it when Melody rebuffed his advances though.

After living with Gil Jr. at the Nelsons' home for a short while, I feared his menacing manner—the way he spoke, acted, and refused to associate with us—and I tiptoed around him. I wasn't alone. All of us foster kids tried to stay clear of him whenever possible, especially as we grew into older teens. We weren't really sure what to make of him, but we knew Gil Jr. didn't make us feel comfortable—specifically Glenn, Charles, and me. He somehow warmed to Darren and took a liking to him. But that wasn't necessarily a good thing.

Gil Jr. became an angry young adult hell-bent on acting out. He grew to be more of a problem for Mr. and Mrs. Nelson with each passing year, until there was nowhere for his unpleasant fury to be hidden. He would lose patience with his mother in front of us kids, and loud shouting matches between Gil Jr. and one or both parents became common. It was all frighteningly out in the open and volatile.

By the age of seventeen, after about ten years of living with us, it was clear that it was him and, increasingly, Gerry, against the world. Whenever he had the chance, and that seemed to be often, he would do something to make our lives miserable. He'd make us clean his room, or bring his laundry downstairs to be washed, or fetch him something from the garage.

"Do it, because I said so," he'd say, meaning every syllable of it. "And do it quickly."

It was sport to him.

There was no mistaking that the air we all breathed became toxic. He moved out in the seventies and moved to California, as far away from his mother as possible. He never came home.

Years later and a lot more clear-sighted, Gil Jr. approached me at his father's funeral. Or more accurately, I went up to him to say hello. I had to know what he thought about all of this. Our living with him, his parents, why did he hate us so?

"She told me she was just bringing one or two kids, temporarily, because they needed help," he said, with a lingering hint of bitterness in his voice, even after all these years. "Then you guys just kept coming and didn't stop. There was no room for me."

Despite of all the abuse I took from him, I understood him. He had a point.

"It wasn't that I hated you personally," he added. "It was just that you were strangers in my house. I resented that."

I think he still does. I never saw him again.

***

Gerry was more oblivious to the negativity of the situation and saw us foster kids as playthings to beat the boredom. He was a good-looking blond boy, loved by all the girls at school. To us, he seemed content and privileged. I wasn't jealous. I was happy for him.

Well, maybe I was a little bit envious as well.

He would typically get involved in family activities like camping and fishing trips, and, unlike Gil Jr., was around most of the time; at least when we were all younger (around ages ten to twelve). Gerry also played sports with us in the backyard, which we wholeheartedly embraced because it got us out of doing chores. At least temporarily.

While Gil Jr. was never part of any of these activities, both fun or otherwise, Gerry and I shared a connection when it came to sports. I had been a baseball and football fan since I was little, and at St. Michael's Home, I had been a pretty good athlete for a six- and seven-year-old. I could run fast; that was my gift. I was also a good baseball player. However, while Gerry liked the Yankees, I was a Mets fan. It was a fan-friendly mutual hatred. We never reconciled that, but we each made scrapbooks of our teams. In 1969, my Mets won the World Series. The Yankees were terrible in those days, and Gerry took out his frustration with the team on me personally. I wound up with either a black eye or a bruised arm. Sometimes both, but nothing permanent.

In the summers, we boys played our own baseball games in the backyard with Gerry, and he always orchestrated the rules. Saying "no" was not an option. Since we didn't have enough kids for a full team and were discouraged by Mrs. Nelson from inviting friends to join, Gerry was usually the batter, but he never ran around the bases; Glenn and I played as the fielders; and either Charles or Darren pitched a regulation-size softball.

No one really wanted to pitch to Gerry for fear of getting hit with the ball. That's because Gerry was a pull-hitter from the left side although he could crush a ball equally well from either side of the plate. He either hit it high and far or he hit it right up the middle. Often it was the later. Charles got nailed the most because he ignored the one rule we all knew to be true: Pitch the ball and don't move. If you pitched him the ball and then ran to the left or right to get out of the way, that's exactly where the ball came hurtling through. Inevitably, Charles would pitch the ball, run left off the pitcher's mound, and get nailed in the leg, side, stomach and other places—but never too seriously. Charles would dance around in pain for a few minutes, and then continue to pitch. We all found it amusing and laughed out loud. (It actually happened a few times to most of us, but not as often as it did to Charles). So, with each at bat, we'd duck if we were the pitcher and retrieve the ball if we were playing in the outfield. We did this over and over again until either we begged Gerry to stop and he finally agreed or it got too dark outside to see.

I had to stand for hours while Gerry batted the ball and

I retrieved it. And boy could he smack the ball. One time, as I stood on a neighbor's driveway some three hundred feet away (we measured by stepping it off with our shoes) from our make-shift home plate under an old swing set without any swings, Gerry practiced batting left-handed. He stroked one over my head and over the neighbor's house. It was impressive...until I had to retrieve the ball from a backyard kiddie pool and got yelled at by that neighbor. When I turned to look, Gerry and the rest of the kids had run and hid. As usual, it was Gerry's fault, but I took the blame.

One time I had injured my left knee during wrestling team practice at school and came home hobbling. I wasn't sure what was wrong, but it hurt severely when I bent it. Gerry insisted I go out and play, but I told him I couldn't; I was in too much pain. I went inside against his wishes and he complained to Mrs. Nelson. She always intervened on Gerry's behalf.

"Walk it off and go out and play with Gerry," she said, without even checking on my leg.

So, I did, but my knee appeared to get worse, and two days later I was in Huntington Hospital having torn cartilage removed from the inside of my knee. I wore a full leg cast for eight weeks and still have a large scar to prove it.

***

Even though I was naturally skilled at baseball, Mrs. Nelson never let me join in the town's organized Little League. She preferred that I stay at home to work around the house. However, thanks to those long "practice sessions" with Gerry, we all became better at baseball than many of the kids in the local Little League. No one could field the ball as well as I could on the school playground, so I always got selected first or second to play on pickup teams at school. Shortstop was my favorite position, and the Mets' Bud Harrelson (who wore number three) was my favorite player.

That backyard also provided us with the opportunity to play with Gil Jr.'s by-then broken-down Hodaka motorcycle. Glenn, Darren, Charles, and I would push each other around the yard on it since the engine didn't work. We had competitions to see who could coast the farthest without falling over. It was tough to maneuver or get any real speed on the uneven lawn, but we managed to have some laughs. There was also an abandoned red Fiat car, infested with hornets' nests that we used to pretend to drive.

We always found things to keep us busy. Being out of sight of Mr. and Mrs. Nelson meant avoiding chores.

***

Later, as we grew up, Gerry became more sadistic and would make us boys do and say whatever he wanted, like little slave boys. He'd sometimes make us do something bad under threat of physical punishment, like steal a baseball from a store or drink something from the kitchen he knew was disgusting like vinegar and apple juice. By obviously favoring him over us, Mrs. Nelson had given him that unspoken right, which we all knew not to dispute.

Darren remembers going to Gerry's room when Darren was ten years old and smoking pot with Gil Jr. and Gerry. Gil Jr. was twenty-two at the time; Gerry was sixteen. Darren was happy to be hanging with the older boys. They, in turn, got a kick out of seeing the young kid stoned. I was fourteen at the time and oblivious to this too-soon milestone event. It was the first time of many, according to Darren. (Darren also secretly started smoking cigarettes with his school friends around this time as well, encouraged by the Nelson boys.)

We all knew that when there was trouble, like when someone broke something, Gerry was never blamed, even when he was at fault. He knew the deal and played it to his advantage. We were also quite aware that Gil Jr. and Gerry were both afforded more privileges than we foster kids were. At the time I don't recall feeling like we were being disrespected or treated unfairly, but, looking back, we were clearly getting the short end of the stick. Gil Jr. and Gerry ate what they wanted and when they wanted; we ate what was offered to us, when it put was out in front of us. Otherwise, the kitchen was closed to us kids. And most frustrating to us, they were allowed to have outside friends come and visit them at the house. We weren't.

7

THE GOOD TIMES

With so many people living under one roof, things could get knotty, but a lengthy, and not always equitable, set of rules kept some semblance of order. Generally, the girls were assigned domestic tasks like cooking and ironing while the boys were instructed to clean the bathroom and kitchen floor. Outside chores were distributed among us all, but mostly to the boys. This seemed reasonable enough until someone refused to do his part.

"I hate scrubbing the floor with a tooth brush," Charles said, with hands red with exhaustion. Then he'd get dramatic. "I can't do it alone. It's too much work."

"Don't look at me," Glenn would quickly say, sensing his help what was sure to be requested. "I have to go weed a bed of poison ivy."

Then Darren walks in and notices Charles mistakenly using his toothbrush to clean the floor.

"That's my toothbrush!" Darren shouted.

"Do you want to help clean the floor?" Charles asked meekly.

"Give me my toothbrush."

Darren wound up cleaning his side of the floor and much of Charles' as well.

Meanwhile Gerry was out by the pond skipping rocks, with not a care in the world. Glenn, Darren, Charles and I all started to take notice of the inequity but said nothing. There was little else to say.

To the outside world our life looked like managed chaos.

In one of his files, an Angel Guardian caseworker at the time noted:

The foster family lives in a large, split-level home which is sometimes in disarray due to the many activities and large number of foster children in the home. The emotional climate in the home is open and sharing, with a display of respect for one another's feelings.

We all came to learn that the more work you did around the house, the more praise you received from Mr. and Mrs. Nelson. That went for both girls and boys. Always trying to get the upper hand over each other, Glenn, Charles, Darren, and I painstakingly dusted the furniture, cleaned the bathrooms and kitchen floors—often with a toothbrush—and dried the dishes after every meal. Outside chores included endlessly weeding of the gardens and trimming the hedges spanning the property line.

Sometimes we fought over who would do what task, depending upon how much manual work was involved, but somehow things always got resolved between us. We knew not to involve the Nelson parents in such decisions. That would mean extra work. Disputes were handled with collective punishment. Everyone payed for one person's smallest misstep.

While the boys did most of the manual work, the girls did much of the cooking and then cleaning the dishes afterward, as well as ironing and dusting. It saved Mrs. Nelson from doing it.

However, Mrs. Nelson washed all of our clothes herself, a formidable task with so many kids, because she didn't want anyone to "touch my machines" for fear of them being broken. To her credit, the machines, both washer and dryer, lasted more than twenty years before new ones needed to be bought.

We all figured out ways of getting around the manual labor and became shrewd at beating the system. It was critical to keeping your sanity and avoiding feeling like a hopeless indentured servant. Sometimes feigning sickness to avoid chores worked—Glenn was a master at this—and sometimes it didn't.

Mrs. Nelson was very strict about how the clothes were to be meticulously pressed and folded. It had to be done "right." Each week the laundry was sorted into two piles that needed to be ironed: one for Kim and one for Melody. With only one iron, Melody always volunteered to iron first because she could do a few articles of clothing and then move the others onto Kim's pile without her knowing it.

One of the jobs we boys particularly hated was drying

the dishes. An old electric dishwasher in the kitchen was always broken, at least as long as I lived there, so every dish, cup and piece of silverware had to be toweled off and put away by hand. While the girls took turns washing, the boys alternated shifts drying. We hated drying because if we were to break a dish, we were hit with a wooden spoon or sent to our room. So, we'd make excuses why we could not do it that particular morning or evening.

To lighten the mood and inject some humor into the situation, I would make fun of someone or something in a not-so-subtle song parody. I was poked fun at plenty of times, as well. That's what made it bearable; we were all subject to playful ridicule. We never minded being the butt of the joke.

Here's one song I wrote around age thirteen in 1973 to the tune of John Kander and Fred Ebb's musical song *Cabaret*, that documents some of the boys' excuses for getting out of drying the dishes.

Drying is something that everyone hates.
Yes, we all hate to dry.
Drying is something we all hate. Yes, we all hate to dry.
When we are playing, it's time to dry.
And when they tell Darren that he dries, he goes upstairs and starts to cry.
Oh, Glenn never dries but what does he care. He says he's got a cold.
Drying is something we all hate.
Yes, we all hate to dry.

Indeed, hard work was a way of life that Mr. and Mrs. Nelson instilled in us foster kids from an early age. A small hokey sign, printed on a rough-cut piece of wood, hung in a prominent spot on the kitchen wall where everyone was sure to see it daily. It read: "All Things Cometh, To Those Who Waiteth, If He Worketh Like Hell While He Waiteth." That message was delivered often, in different ways, loud and clear. It was the very backbone of who Mr. and Mrs. Nelson were. The harder you worked the better person you were.

When it wasn't a school day, everyone was given a daily task, except the Nelsons' sons. While we were busy with our assignments, it seemed Gil Jr. and Gerry never had to do anything they didn't want to. All us foster kids came to hate this and often commiserated among ourselves, but we never dared argue about it with Mr. or Mrs. Nelson.

That's just the way it was.

***

"Little Guys, get down here now!"

Both menacing and comforting at the same time, that's a phrase that has stayed with me forever. It was the all too-familiar, booming sound of Melody's voice summoning us to gather at the bottom of the stairs or in the kitchen. It was used either to call us all to a meal or because a family proclamation was in store—typically, one or more of us was in trouble. The tone and volume of Melody's bellow usually signaled which was which. Either way, you had to show your face.

If you had done something wrong, everyone was witness to the punishment. That could be physical with a wooden spoon across the butt or a verbal tongue-lashing.

We all watched the punishments but didn't really want to.

Somehow it felt welcome that she always started with the "little guys." But she soon followed with, "Mike! Glenn! I don't want to have to tell you twice. I'm not kidding around. Come to dinner now!"

We always obeyed. As I said earlier, you heeded the reveille and came running. It was kind of like the father of the Von Trapp family beckoning his kids with a whistle. Instead of a whistle, though, we had Melody's piercing scream of a voice.

Melody was Mrs. Nelson's chosen triggerman and as such, she did most of the verbal dirty work. Whenever Mrs. Nelson needed us to do something, she didn't request it herself; she'd get Melody to do so. I think secretly Melody relished the role. It put her in charge. She wasn't pretty, had scraggly red hair, couldn't hear well and wore old cat's-eye glasses, but she was the boss. No one ever challenged her authority. When Melody told you to do something, you did it.

***

There's a silver lining to everything, even if mine was harder to find. Mr. Nelson's unrelenting busy work kept me out of his hair and occupied. If I wasn't doing something constructive for him, I was probably up to no good. That's how he thought. Whenever he was working on an old car or rearranging the garage, he would come calling for me. He would give me a task, and then leave me alone for a few hours to complete it. Andy was treated exactly the same way years earlier; I was simply the latest in line.

And busy work it was. There were times when I was told to clean the garage, then Mr. Nelson would mess it up with a variety of new things—an old car without an engine, some used tires, or simply boxes of "stuff"—and I'd have to clean and organize it all over again. I rearranged the garage more times than I can remember.

There was the time Mr. Nelson decided that I should hang every tool he owned, and there were roughly two hundred, on one wall of the garage. This, he said, would allow him to find what he needed quickly. I was instructed to paint the wall a light blue, hang the screwdrivers, hammers, wrenches and other assorted tools with two nails each, and then trace an outline of every tool. Next, he had me color in each outline in red. This way, when a tool was missing, you'd see the red space and know the tool was out of place immediately. It was actually a good idea, but it took me about two weeks to complete. This angered Mr. Nelson because he thought it should have been done more quickly and he told me so.

"You know, this doesn't have to take all day," he chastised.

I always wanted to please him, so I did the next job much faster. He'd praise me by giving me another job to do.

"You did a good job," he'd say, making it sound like an award, "I think you can handle the attic."

To his credit, however, as hard as we toiled around the house or outside it, Mr. Nelson worked equally hard himself. He led by example, so our complaining felt futile. Except for a one-week family vacation every year, Mr. Nelson worked in New York City as a computer service technician and commuted during the week, and then worked on cars and other projects every weeknight and weekend day.

Up until I was about fifteen, we went to church each Sunday morning, then came home and worked in the yard (or garage in the winter). When I wasn't assigned a specific chore, my job was to stand or sit at Mr. Nelson's side and give him whatever tool he needed.

He wasn't a good step-by-step guy and really didn't have the knack (or patience) for teaching. I had to figure it out by myself. "I'm going to teach you how to be a man," he'd often say, but he never really showed me how to do anything. What he meant was that I needed to know how to use tools to fix things. But instead of giving me helpful instruction, it was made clear that I was there just to assist, to learn by watching. I was there to hand him the wrench but was not allowed to loosen the bolt.

I learned never to touch what he was working on, unless asked. If I handed him the wrong tool, or mistakenly installed a part backwards, he would bark, "What's the matter with you?" That phrase was said to me so many times, there was a point when I questioned if there was actually something wrong with me. *Maybe I wasn't so smart.*

As I grew to be sixteen, I forced myself to enjoy doing these projects. I learned in the orphanage that there was always "fun" amongst the rubble. Undesirable things can be endured and navigated. I became good at finding the silver lining and I was putting it to good use.

What else was I to do? I knew physical labor made the Nelsons happy, and I began to eagerly throw myself into the wide variety of jobs Mr. Nelson undertook. He was an eager DIY (do-it-yourself) proponent; replacing an electric starter with a taped-up jumper wire on a car one day, fixing the blower in the dryer with mismatched screws the next, and then building a wooden bookcase from materials found on the side of the road after that. Sometimes he'd cover many projects all in the same day. With his engineering background, there wasn't anything Mr. Nelson couldn't make or fix. He often jury-rigged things with string or mismatched screws to miraculously make them operate properly. Once he plugged a hole in a car radiator with a piece of plumber's putty. Another time he sewed two pieces of aluminum roof flashing together with rusty steel baling wire. The result wasn't always pretty to look at, but it almost always worked.

In many facets, he was a man's man from the 1950's. He taught me many things, including how to be a man. But he did it without wanting to.

***

Mr. Nelson loved the notion of acquiring things he didn't have to pay for and never missed an opportunity for free stuff. It was like a game to him, and us kids made it happen, without complaining. Our little work detail of Glenn, Charles, Darren and I gathered all sorts of free stuff that he had secured from local vegetable or dairy farmers. This included gathering cow manure for the vegetable garden, which we'd pick up with broken shovels—found by the side of the road—by cleaning out the local farmer's (Pete Sobel) cow barns. We'd load up several five-gallon drums in a car and then ride home, with the car windows open, amid the pails of smelly bovine shit and its all-consuming odor.

Per Mr. Nelson's instruction, the animal waste would later be mixed with water and left to steep for a week in large steel drums before we'd water the garden plants with this "manure tea." Despite our disgust, his method was sound: this nitrogen-rich tea made the tomatoes, cucumbers, squash and every other vegetable grow twice as big as in previous years and resulted in an abundance of all types.

Of course, during these excursions there was always one of us who would disrupt the embarrassment of this dung-filled humiliation by saying something painfully obvious.

"Did someone fart?"

We'd all howl with laughter, which made us feel better about the "yucky" (Kim's word) situation.

But we were just doing what we were told. There were times in the evening after school that we'd get driven to a local field and gather free corn left unpicked, being careful to avoid the bug-infested ears. There were burlap bags for each of us, and we'd typically fill about four each before we had finished for the evening. We often ate some of the corn as we picked and got stomachaches from eating too many.

"You ought to put some of that corn in the bag," Mr. Nelson would admonish upon seeing us munching an uncooked ear.

"The corn is not going to pick itself."

After you overcame the idea of eating raw corn, it tasted sweet. I remember the fragrant smell and freshness of that corn in the field.

***

Speaking of corn, among his many interests, Mr. Nelson was fascinated with Native American farming methods. He told us that even though the Indians didn't have a lot to eat, they would always surrender parts of their fish harvests to the gods to ensure a good crop. So, like they had done for hundreds of years, we'd use two-person dragnets to gather minnows from the Long Island Sound. This fish were in turn used as fertilizer for the garden. As instructed, we'd put three small fishes in each hole when planting vegetable plants to make them grow bigger and yield more fruit. It really worked.

Like many in the '70s, Mr. Nelson was also a big proponent of recycling. Nowadays everyone talks about being "green" and saving the planet, but back then Mr. Nelson decried pollution and was heavily into renewable energy (mainly water and wind power), repurposing or recycling many household staples (salt could be used for removing stains in clothing and as mouthwash when you had a sore throat, and baking soda made for an effective, if distasteful, toothpaste), and living off the land. He'd get outlandish ideas after voraciously reading an issue of *Mother Earth News* magazine, and the next thing I knew, I was helping him build compost boxes for the garden or a small windmill. We never really used the windmill for anything practical, but we proved we could pump small amounts of water with wind power. We actually did it.

We'd also reclaim unwanted used wooden sheds—discarded on the side of the road or in someone's backyard—which had to be taken down piece by piece, driven over to the Nelsons' house in an overloaded truck, and then reassembled in the Nelson's yard. The sheds were used for storage of things we didn't really need to save—an old water heater, a couple of bicycle frames with no wheels, and rusted pieces of sheet metal from an old roof—but Mr. Nelson believed that everything could or would have value one day.

We salvaged about five sheds, until we had too many for the available space to bear. But that didn't stop Mr. Nelson. When we ran out of room, we simply stacked the wood pieces in piles for "another day." Eventually, we never assembled them, which created a veritable junkyard on the side of the house.

When referring to discarded items he instructed us to pick up from the side of the road, he never used the word "junk." Instead he'd describe it as "good stuff." He figured he would either use the parts around the house or sell them for extra money at the Saturday flea market held in the parking lot of the local drive-in theater. We went to that market every week for about a year in the spring and summer months when I was sixteen years old.

We would drive around town in a large flatbed truck when certain neighborhoods were encouraging residents to throw away large unwanted objects on specific days of the week. We called these "Junk Days," although we'd typically travel around at night so no one would see us. Mr. Nelson drove the truck while Glenn, Charles, Darren, and I rode in the back. You had to hold on tight or risk getting bumped off.

After a few weeks of this, we got it down to a science and were able to work quickly. When an item was spotted, Mr. Nelson would stop the truck. Two of us would jump down and retrieve an old water heater—the lead lining inside was valuable, we were told—or a wrought iron gate and hand it up to the third and fourth person. We'd repeat this about ten times an outing. Metal was money, so we couldn't miss an opportunity or "a single piece of salvage-able material," Mr. Nelson would say.

We'd also make weekly visits to the local Helping Hand Rescue Mission at night, after the place was closed, and gather the garbage that had been thrown to the curb. My stomach still gets nauseous when I think about it. Mr. Nelson instructed us to pick up the garbage bags, bring them home, and then go through them in the basement to look for valuable items—old shoes, women's pocketbooks, toys, clothes, etc. We were picking through half-eaten food and other unmentionables that even a secondhand charity shop didn't want. Yet, we did as we were told; we collected it, held our noses to avoid the smell, and brought it home to store with the mounting piles of used items in the Nelsons' basement.

After a few months of this, we had accumulated large amounts of shoes, toys, and other discarded items that were lined up in neat piles. The plan was to sell these things, but it never fully materialized because every time a potential buyer at the flea market would try to negotiate a lower price, Mr. Nelson refused to budge and wouldn't sell it for less. Then we'd have to cart the stuff back home and hope for the best the following week. The windfall never came and the good stuff piled up higher and higher.

After a while, Mr. Nelson somehow lost interest and stopped taking us to the flea market. It was that way with a lot of schemes Mr. Nelson concocted to bring more money into the household. He'd get us all to begin a lengthy and involved undertaking and then abruptly stop, sometimes for good reason and sometimes not. The real reasons were his and his alone. Meanwhile those shoes and pocketbooks were still in the basement long after I left the Nelsons for college. They were eventually thrown out when Mr. and Mrs. Nelson died and the house was sold.

However harsh, all of these "missions," as we liked to call them, gave us kids a shared sense of being in it together, no matter what else in the world was happening. At times, it felt to me as if these outings were shameful and literally pitted us against the world. Who else would even think of doing this? Our only hope was that none of our friends from school ever saw us or knew about what we were doing. It was stressful, keeping these secrets, but also nurtured a lot of camaraderie when we were in the moment.

***

One day, in the fall of 1977, I was sitting in my high school English class listening to the teacher read aloud my essay on migrant workers and the hardships they endured. It was part of an assignment after we had read John Steinbeck's book *The Grapes of Wrath*. The teacher used all sorts of praise to describe how precisely my "Diary of a Migrant Worker" described the challenges the book's characters overcame. She didn't know, because I didn't tell her, that the "lifelike artistic representation" and "truthful experience" she found in my paper were actually what we kids had done a week earlier in the evenings after school. Mr. Nelson had gotten a local farmer to agree to allow us to salvage potatoes left on the ground after the harvesting machine had come through. All of us kids, including the girls but not Gerry and Gilbert, were taken at dusk to a large dirt field that was littered with thousands of small potatoes the size of golf balls. We were instructed to pick only whole potatoes, not ones that had cuts or bruises from the farmer's harvester.

We'd load up the family Volkswagen minibus, with the center seat taken out, with five-gallon plastic buckets filled with potatoes and then take them home to be washed and stored in the garage. We ate potatoes that entire winter, in many forms: stewed, mashed, baked, fried, peeled, and unpeeled. By the time spring rolled around, we hated potatoes. That's also when the remaining potatoes grew "eyes" (sprouts), turned green, and became inedible.

These "pickings" were endured with tomfoolery in order to get through them. Throwing a few "bad" potatoes at Glenn's head often did the trick. He would return fire and try to get Charles and Darren to join his side. This would usually end with an admonishment from Mr. Nelson, but the fun provided the release we needed.

In my school paper I had written about the dirt under the fingernails of the exhausted workers, how it got there and how long it stayed on their hands, even after repeated washings. As my teacher glowingly read my paper, I smiled and looked down at the dirt under my own fingernails. Steinbeck had chronicled our similar migrant farmworker conditions perfectly, although it wasn't fiction; it was my life.

***

Mr. Nelson also taught us about airplanes and how basic aeronautics worked. His magazine subscription to *Popular Science* helped. However, while I was fascinated, Glenn was only mildly interested, and Gerry had no interest whatsoever. We all went along with it, although Charles and Darren were not included. Within weeks of first discussing it, Gerry was given a Piper Cub plane kit, with precut wooden parts, parchment covering for the wings and body, and an extremely small gas prop engine. It also had a remote unit with a telescoping antenna to control the plane's ailerons and flaps in flight. Mr. Nelson helped Gerry fly the plane, and it was a sight to see as it took off and flew smoothly through the land and landed safely after a few minutes of flight.

I got four pieces of quarter-inch by eight-inch wide raw balsa wood and a set of blueprint plans Mr. Nelson had brought home from work that included having to cut the wings and other parts out of the balsa wood by hand. Oh, and mine didn't have an engine.

"Mike, you're going to build a glider," Mr. Nelson said, with emphasis on the word *glider*. Seeing me frown he quickly added, "Don't worry about what Gerry got. People fly gliders too."

So, I followed the plans closely and began to build this plane out of balsa wood. I spent a month working on it, using sharp Exacto knives that often led to bleeding. After I had painstakingly cut, sculpted, and assembled the pieces and carefully sanded the surfaces to the correct aerodynamic proportions (as described by my Guillow's home building kit plans), I proudly took it outside in the back yard so Mr. Nelson and several of the kids could watch me launch it. I tossed it hard. It went up, lost lift, and quickly came crashing down into a pile of rubble. I was devastated. All that work was now a pile of splintered balsa wood.

Without helping to pick up the pieces, Mr. Nelson said to me, "Build it again," and I did. And once again, weeks later, it crashed after a very short flight. He got annoyed and said he couldn't deal with my lack of model-building skills anymore.

"You're never going to get this," he said, exasperated after a few failed flights.

"What's wrong with you?"

Much of the time Mr. Nelson had little patience for us kids if we didn't do a job right the first time. He didn't like "dillydallying," as he put it. This impatience sometimes led to his knocking us out of the way, literally, when we happened to be in his path. He once stepped on Darren's foot when Darren didn't move fast enough. That's what he got for dillydallying. Mr. Nelson treated all of us boys, but not the girls, the same. The girls got special treatment. Mr. Nelson taught us to respect women and give him the right of way.

It made us light on our feet.

"You gotta move, get outta my way," he'd sternly say, and he wasn't kidding.

"Children should be seen and not heard" was another favorite expression. Yes, he actually said that many times, and Mrs. Nelson heartily agreed.

"Sometimes it's best not to say anything," she said, echoing his sentiment. "You might learn something."

***

When we were not doing chores, the house, backyard, and surrounding area served as an unlimited playground, full of possibilities for a young kid. Left to our own devices, we'd build forts out of scrap wood, cardboard boxes and pieces of fabric; play war games with sticks substituting for guns; and have hilarious and sometimes injurious slipper fights in our room at night in the dark.

At bedtime, Darren, Charles, Glenn, and I would gather dozens of lightweight foam flip-flop sandals from around the house and hide them under our bed covers. Then we'd turn off the light, wait a beat, and after one of us yelled "slipper fight!!" begin throwing them indiscriminately at one another. As luck would have it, someone always got hit in the face, but the shoes were mostly made of foam so no one ever required stitches. We'd repeat this game several times a night until Mrs. Nelson heard the slippers bouncing off the walls, door, and ceiling and yelled out for us to stop.

Muffled laughter and more slippers being thrown in the dark brought more of Mrs. Nelson's ire: "Stop that damn noise and go to sleep!"

It took several cycles of this before we actually fell asleep, we were having too much fun. I never had this type of companionship at St. Michael's. It was wonderful.

***

We also gave each other nicknames that we'd use for teasing around the house. Kim was "Kimba" after the Japanese anime TV series *Kimba the White Lion*. Melody was "Mookie" because as a child she would ask for milk by saying "I want mook." I was "Picalino" because one day Mrs. Nelson was kidding around and called out to me, saying "Hey, Picalino Morico Gratso," which didn't really make sense and still doesn't today, but it stuck. Glenn was

"Keebler" after the famous cookie-making elves in the television commercials—Glenn and the elves shared similarly pointy ears. Charles was "Pinko Chinko" because he had Chinese-looking eyes—racist, I know, but we kids didn't think about things like that then. Darren was known as "Weiner," a name given him by Gil Jr., who sometimes called him a little wiener due to Darren's small size.

The other kids—Gil Jr., Rose Ann, and Andy—didn't have such monikers, although Mrs. Nelson called Gerry "Dinkleberry" because it rhymed with his name and I believe she wanted him to join in the fun. Of course, we were afraid to call Gerry by his nickname, but we used these names to poke fun at one another often.

We invented lots of fun things to do in those days, as long as they didn't require money. We'd hold makeshift country fairs in the backyard that only we attended, complete with a rock band and fake instruments and novelty games like "pitch the ball in the apple picker" and bowling on the grass.

Glenn and I once went to the nearby pond and challenged each other to see who could catch the most fish (mainly catfish and sunfish) with worms from the garden. We started around ten on a Saturday morning and didn't leave until the sun went down.

"You're catching the same fish over and over again," Glenn said to me, caught up in the "serious" rivalry.

"So are you," I responded, noticing the multiple hook marks on the spiny catfish he'd just reeled in. I think we were equally guilty and our determination to best each other was real.

"I'm beating your ass," he said, and in the end he was right. Using worms from the garden, I caught seventy-five fish, while Glenn caught seventy-eight. Yes, it was that close. But in the end, it didn't matter who won. We threw them all back into the water anyway.

Another time we were taken to an all-you-can-eat Saturday morning pancake breakfast fundraiser at the church we attended. We decided to see who could eat the most. While we all tried our hardest, Darren, then the smallest of us all, ate twice as many pancakes (twenty-three, although today he swears it was more) as anyone else. When we got home, some thirty minutes later, he was hungry again.

Other times, when Mrs. Nelson wasn't looking, we would make strange concoctions in the kitchen. We called them cocktails—combinations of things like sugar, flour, powered milk and the flavored water remaining at the bottom of the pot after steaming vegetables—and invariably pressured Darren to drink them. He always did, and then ran around like a crazy person to make us all laugh. Darren grew up to have the biggest and strongest body among us. At one point in his life, he was a competitive bodybuilder. We now joke that it was those famous cocktails that did the trick.

"Who had the last laugh," Darren now gloats, flexing his thirteen-inch biceps.

8

RIDING THE BUS

Mr. Nelson loved the outdoors. While he was a staunch advocate for hard work and elbow grease, he also felt it important to take time out for family vacations and spending time in nature. That is, when he didn't have a job for us to do.

Growing up, he always reminded me of someone in a Norman Rockwell painting, complete with kooky facial expression, red plaid shirt, and fishing hat with a variety of lures stuck into it. He also smoked a pipe for a year or so, but one day Mrs. Nelson informed him that smoking was a bad influence on the children and ordered him to give it up. He readily did.

Before Rose Ann, Charles, and I joined the household, the Nelsons regularly went on family camping and boating trips that included Gil Jr. and Gerry. They bought a large tent, and then later a small boat to use in the waters off Long Island. The kids were instructed never to wear shoes on the boat, for fear of scratching the deck. By the time I moved into the house, in 1969, Gil Jr. had stopped participating in family outings, and the boat had become a wasp-infested relic discarded at the side of the house.

Between 1970 and 1974, the once-a-year trips (now including Rose Ann, Charles, and me) continued, but to different places than the Nelsons had been before. These excursions had to be approved by my biological father, who agreed in written form. We traveled to the annual Kutztown Fair, in Pennsylvania's Amish country, where we'd go on rides, eat shoofly pie, and watch tractor-pull competitions.

At the fair, we also would dare one another to drink the blood from a slaughtered pig. Up on a stage, two men would hang a large live specimen from a big steel hook, as it writhed and struggled to free itself. One of the men would then kill the animal by slitting its throat with a large knife, right before the audience's eyes, and then invite anyone to come up and try a sip, catching the fresh blood in a paper cup as it dripped down and pooled on the floor below. No one I know ever drank that warm blood, not even Darren who would try anything. The horror of killing that big creature upside down was atrocious to me. I could barely watch the proceedings and covered my eyes with my hands for most of it. I couldn't help but see the blood, however, especially after the carnival man on stage shocked the audience by drinking it himself (or claiming to). That turned my stomach—and I'm sure everyone else's—every time.

As a family, we'd also travel to Nickerson Park in upstate New York and camp in a pop-up camper that slept eight (although hot and uncomfortably). At night we'd sit around a campfire and roast marshmallows. Some of the best parts of living with the Nelsons were these outings, filled with fishing, hiking, laughing, and togetherness.

About two years after we all outgrew the pop-up camper, Mr. Nelson decided to upgrade to a larger vehicle. Ever resourceful, he bought an old GMC school bus and was determined to convert it into a mobile home. In a bit of bad luck, the engine on that bus blew a piston after only a few months, so we had to replace the old engine with a newer one. That entailed setting up a winch-and-pulley system (designed by Mr. Nelson), and then Glenn, Darren, and I leaning with all our might on that winch to help Mr. Nelson lift the engine into place. It was tough work, and we spent three days doing it. Unfortunately, that engine was a dud as well, and Mr. Nelson wound up with a hernia in his groin that required surgery.

Concluding that we needed a new project, the Nelsons demanded that we work on the school bus virtually night and day. Mr. Nelson also decided that he didn't want the neighbors to see what we were doing, so he had Glenn and me build a ten-foot wooden fence around the bus on one side of the house. Mr. Nelson drew up a plan and helped us lay out the frame. Then he left Glenn and me to have at it with a saw, nails, and a hammer. We cut all the boards with a hand saw. It was tough work, and we were promised a lobster dinner after we finished. We completed it in about a week—sometimes toiling until after dark—but never got that lobster dinner. I don't think we liked lobster at that age.

Once the fence was completed, Mr. Nelson supervised while Glenn, Darren, and I worked inside the bus, tearing out all the seats. He considered Charles "useless," and thus he rarely asked him to help when manual labor was involved. We also had to dismantle the sheet-metal side panels to prepare for a new interior, working without a clue as to what we were actually doing.

The day after we removed the final interior side panel of that old school bus, Mr. Nelson drove up in a newer and larger 1974 Blue Bird/Ford school bus. I was told to reattach all the side panels to the older bus because it had been traded as part of the new deal. I worked alone through the night with a flashlight and got all the panels reattached with hand-snapped aluminum rivets in two days. Mr. Nelson seemed impressed by my efforts and genially shook my hand to congratulate me. And he had a smile on his face, something I was not accustomed to. It made me feel proud, useful and...wanted. That feeling lasted about ten minutes, as Mr. Nelson snapped me back to reality by telling me to get to work on the new bus.

"We've really got to do this right," he said. "Don't make any plans. There's more work to do."

Mr. Nelson frenetically began drawing the designs for the inside of that new Ford school bus. It would be bigger and better than his original plans. The new design might have been considered overkill, since he used one-inch steel tubing instead of wood two-by-fours for the internal structural framing, but that was Mr. Nelson's style. Always overbuild to ensure it lasts over time, he'd say. This meticulous attention to detail came from his engineering background and was always preaching the right and wrong ways to do things. That might include the way you held a hammer.

"Not too high on the handle," he'd say, "you want to get leverage to drive that nail home!"

Glenn and I got so good at it, we could pound a nail into a piece of wood with two swings. It was part of yet another competition between us.

Mr. Nelson's wildly optimistic vision also required Glenn and I to learn how to use a propylene-gas industrial welding torch so that we could cut the metal pieces and secure them together to create the mobile home's steel infrastructure. Glenn and I were not welders by any measure, but we burned our fingers many times and learned what not to do by trial and error. There was always a dare between us to see who could stare longest at the blue flame without wearing the dark-coated protective welder's goggles. That's because we were told that if you stared at the flame for too long, you would go blind. Of course, being young and curious, we had to see if that was true.

Sometimes Glenn stared longer, other times I did. Both of us can see now, so I guess whatever eye damage we suffered wasn't serious. And the burn marks from that hot flame are long gone too.

Once Glenn accidentally set fire to the insulation inside one of the metal side panels of the bus and the entire interior filled with putrid gray smoke, so we had to evacuate fast. We were afraid Mr. Nelson would find out, so we didn't tell anyone as we scurried to put out the fire. Unfortunately, all we had were two small cups and a garden hose that was too short to reach the bus, so we repeatedly refilled those cups and ran back and forth like the Keystone Kops until the fire was extinguished. The smell of fire did not get past Mr. Nelson, and he scolded us for almost destroying the bus. He never asked if we were okay.

The fire set us back about three days, because we had to wait for the odor to dissipate. Then we were back at work, nascent welders that we were. After three months, the resulting mobile home/bus was—to my easily astounded mind—an engineering marvel. It accommodated a dozen people comfortably and included a dining area with two matching retractable tables at the rear, a kitchen and bathroom along each side in the middle, and enough beds for everyone. All available internal and undercarriage space was used as efficiently as possible—every seat on the bus (except the driver's) doubled as a storage bin or bed. Under the body, the bus carried two large water tanks, a septic tank (installed mostly with the help of Darren, then ten years old), and a propane tank—making the motor home completely self-sustaining.

We could (and did several times) pull into a parking lot and set up for a few days; all we required was a source of AC power. At night, the two tables became beds.

It all began with a Rube Goldberg-style idea hatched inside Mr. Nelson's head.

The bus was nearly finished—some interior walls were not complete, and the outside had not been painted—when we began taking it on trips to Freeport, Maine (sleeping in the L.L.Bean parking lot was a favorite stop) and Nova Scotia, Canada. The exhilaration of seeing Canada's most famous Roman Catholic Church, the Basilica of Sainte-Anne-de-Beauprè in Quebec, has stayed with me forever. It was like the Emerald City in the movie "The Wizard Of Oz," high atop a long flight of steps.

The most interesting part to me, however, was learning that this massive stone church contains fragments of the bones of Saint Anne, enshrined in a glass box. It was creepy looking at those bones, but I found it fascinating, nonetheless. I wondered if they were really her bones. There were also hundreds of stairs to climb to get into the church, which we kids did repeatedly, racing each other up and down, just to pass the time.

Owing to Mrs. Nelson's religious-zealot bent, the Basilica of Sainte-Anne-de-Beauprè became a semiannual journey, maybe even a pilgrimage, for three years. We never discussed it beforehand. We simply loaded into the bus and went.

***

There were scary times when we collectively willed the bus up steep mountain inclines, the steel frame and wood paneling creaking with tension and strain. We also held our breath going downhill as Mr. Nelson pulled hard on the hand brake to keep the bus from free-falling down the mountains. This caused us to stare anxiously at each other, speechless, fearing doom and forgetting all about the beautiful mountainous scenery that was passing by outside.

One time we were traveling on the bus through Maine on our way to Canada, when two police cars pulled us over. We were not speeding, because Mr. Nelson never drove faster than fifty miles per hour. Normally, we moved a lot slower, as the weight of the vehicle made the old engine literally spit and sputter as we climbed up the long winding mountain roads. It took Mr. Nelson a good fifteen minutes before he could negotiate the bus to the side of the highway, the police in extremely slow pursuit.

We finally pulled over and two stern officers came on board. After an informal search of the interior, they told us we could not drive on state roads because the bus was painted yellow and black and we were obviously not associated with any school district. It wasn't street legal.

The officers were abrupt and said we'd have to evacuate immediately and leave the bus where it was. Mr. Nelson spoke at length with one of the officers and convinced him to let us paint over the black parts of the bus in order to comply with the rules and continue our journey. We had exactly one day, the cops said, and they would be back to see if we had complied.

Since the police would not allow us to drive the bus to get the paint, several of us hiked two miles along the side of the highway until we came to a hardware store. We bought two-dozen cans of brown spray paint and everyone in the family was given a can. For the next few hours, we painted over everything on the outside of the bus that was black, including the bumpers, side stripes and many other areas. This required us to hang out one of the windows to reach the high spots, risking an eight-foot fall. I reached up as far as my arms would go, while Melody held my legs as a I stood on the window ledge, with my back to the ground. We repeated that move fourteen times (that's how many windows are on a typical school bus) with our shoes wedged tight against the window frame, and luckily no one fell. We finished just as the sun was going down. The next day we all laughed at how ugly it looked in the daylight. It was mostly yellow, with a chaotic splattering of brown spots in strategic places. It wasn't pretty, but it passed the policemen's inspection, and we were on our way.

When we got back home after the trip, we all helped paint the entire exterior powder blue, with a white top. The curious color scheme was Mrs. Nelson's idea. This time, over a weekend, we used an electric paint sprayer and compressor, which made the job a lot easier. When we finished, it looked pretty good. It was ready for another journey.

However, all of us kids had small specks of light blue paint in our hair, which caused the school nurse to think we had head lice the following Monday, and she said we could not come back to school until the problem had resolved. It took a bit of negotiation on Mrs. Nelson's part to convince them otherwise and, after careful reinspection by the school nurse, we were allowed back in school.

As a finishing touch, Mr. Nelson, using his impressive artistic skills, hand-painted caricature images along the side of the bus to represent each one of us, including our two dogs, Happy and Melody. The boys were represented by cartoonish boy profiles, the girls were painted as young females with brown ponytails, and the dogs were drawn with their tongues hanging out. It made for quite the spectacle, and wherever we traveled, strangers made remarks about the bus and its bohemian style. We were a novelty reminiscent of television's "The Partridge Family," but more authentic and ethnically diverse.

Traveling in the bus was always an adventure because it got us out of the house and required that we live and work together closely, as a family unit. I suggested putting an eight-track player in the bus so we could listen to music. I had seen an advertisement on TV and was spell bound.

To my young mind, listening to music without using a turntable—something that was too expensive for me—was a "wow" moment. Of course, the player costs twice what a small record player did, but it was the future.

Mrs. Nelson initially fought against this. She said she was against "modern" music and to her, radios—and now eight-track players, heaven forbid—in cars were a distraction for the driver. The new music could make you crash. Thankfully, Mr. Nelson conceded since I had done so much work on the bus. However, I didn't have any of the tapes. So, Mrs. Nelson went to the record store and inexplicably bought two eight-track cassettes that could not have been more different. One was the soundtrack to Rodgers and Hammerstein's *The Sound of Music* (for her), and she gave me the Bill Withers album *Still Bill*, featuring the hit song "Lean On Me."

I had never heard of Bill Withers before, so why she thought I would like it is still a mystery to me. Of all the eight-track cassettes in the world, Mrs. Nelson picked that Withers album, with the song "Lean On Me."

As I look back now, the lyrics seem appropriate for the situation. How telling it was, about all of our hard-time pasts and hopeful futures.

> *Sometimes in our lives, we all have pain.*
> *We all have sorrow.*
> *But if we are wise, we know that there's*
> *Always tomorrow*

On the bus we all happily sang along with the Von Trapp family, but the Withers album was another thing altogether. I listened intently as it played in the background while we traveled along but I'm not sure anyone else did. No one sang along; for us it wasn't really that type of record. But I heard it, and for many times later the words loudly circulated endlessly in my head. Sometimes it was hard to make it stop.

9

MAKING THE HOLIDAYS

Mrs. Nelson's autocratic rule during the rest of the year was suspended when the holidays rolled around. We looked forward to the holidays all year long because they were magic in every sense of the word. Whatever troubles you had vanished when it was time for a holiday, and all of us—including Gerry but not Gil Jr.—helped to make them special. For everyone in the family, the days leading up to each holiday were a welcome breathing space from the typical unease.

It was literally something to lick one's lips over.

The Catholic holidays, specifically Christmas and Easter, were meticulously prepared events in the Nelson house, filled with food and festive decorations. At Christmas there were dozens of fake plastic poinsettia plants and homemade decorations to place around the living room and cotton blankets for snow under the tree and on table top. The days leading up to Easter saw us hanging homemade egg-themed art literally everywhere. It was meticulous work, but worth the effort.

"You have to make the holiday; it doesn't make itself," Mrs. Nelson would say each year, and I still believe that to this day. Creating and the build-up to the actual day was half the fun.

No one put more effort into making them special than Mrs. Nelson. On Christmas Eve, Mrs. Nelson worked for days prior with Kim and Melody in the kitchen to prepare a huge feast. The smells filling the house were euphoric for days.

Owing to Italian tradition to refrain from eating red meat on the eve of a feast day, the Christmas Eve meal included stuffed calamari (squid, complete with the tentacles), snails in tomato sauce, anchovies and spaghetti, and chicken cacciatore. There was also a thin spaghetti dish made of whole breaded anchovies and cheese. I hated the taste of anchovies as much as the stuffed squid, but we ate it all and came to love every second of those meals. These were the times to celebrate as a family, and we did.

On Christmas mornings, we'd wake up early—one year Darren didn't sleep the night before—to the sight of a brightly glowing tree covered in ornaments, some we made others were store bought, and the sounds of Andy Williams singing Christmas songs. Presents for the boys included new underwear and socks, along with a shared toy like a remote-control race car set. However meager, it was the utterly welcome opposite of what holidays were like in my younger days in Queens or later at St. Michael's.

The feeling was hypnotic.

On Easter, there would be eight baskets of candy lined up along the living room fireplace. Mrs. Nelson, with the help of Melody and Kim, would pack and wrap them in colored cellophane the night before. We'd all salivate at the sight of candy but were not allowed to eat any until after we returned from church. Then we'd come home and dig in, often trading candy with each other to get more of our favorite ones. This late morning sugar feast was followed in the afternoon by baked ham on the dinner table.

For our part of the celebration, we boys—minus Gerry and Gil Jr.— performed variety shows at the top of the long staircase in the living room, including a series of comical sketches and some musical numbers. Our props included things we found around the house, like a sock puppets, fake glasses, musical instruments (both homemade and real), a rubber chicken and a pair of boys tighty-whitey underwear with the word "NEWS" scrawled across the back.

I wrote all the material that we performed. The girls, Mr. and Mrs. Nelson, and any relatives who happened to be visiting would make up the audience. One "News Briefs" segment was introduced by Darren holding up the underwear. Picture Glenn at sixteen, and Darren, age twelve, sitting behind a fake news desk (two chairs positioned backwards and covered with a sheet) delivering the following bit. It was part of a live newscast from our 1976 Christmas Eve show. It poked fun at everyone in the family... except Mr. and Mrs. Nelson and Gil Jr. It was always best to stay away from them with the jokes.

These descriptions lampoon each one of our foibles at the time. (Note: I never lampooned myself.)

And now we introduce this year's "Voted Most Likely to…" Awards. We've compiled a list of the people most likely to succeed at nothing at all. Sure, they're ugly and belong in jail, but who are we to pass judgment?

Kim…most likely to have ten kids, then forget three of them in a shopping mall.

Gerry…most likely to find Glenn's broken models (which Gerry broke) in the attic and break them again.

Glenn…most likely to tell on Michael, then do the same thing Michael did when no one is looking.

Melody…most likely to lose weight and get carried away in a windstorm.

Charlie…most likely to use an entire box of tissues crying over spilt milk.

Darren…most likely to pluck his eyelashes out and have no facial hair.

January 6 was a religious holiday we called "Little Christmas." It's more commonly known in the Catholic tradition as the Feast of the Epiphany—the day when Christ supposedly revealed himself to mankind (or something like that). Occurring twelve days after Christmas, some also use the day to celebrate the arrival of the three wise men who followed a star to visit the baby Jesus in Bethlehem. We'd celebrate with food and small gifts—typically more underwear and socks.

During the evening we would perform a puppet show taken from a religious book the Nelsons had us read from each year. It involves a Catholic priest, portrayed by a white sock puppet, admonishing Black Peter, a brown sock puppet. Both sock puppets had holes cut out so your fingers could serve as arms. In the script, Black Peter giggles a lot, thinks bad thoughts, and does wicked things. It was a morality play whose message I don't quite recall in detail, but we performed it faithfully (excuse the pun) for many years. I mostly played the part of Black Peter because Mrs. Nelson liked the squeaky voice I used.

There was a summer festival we threw for ourselves one year, to which no one else came, and I remember a St. Patrick's Day show as well. Our performances, comically off key and very rough, were limited but great family fun.

However, getting the boys through the show without hysterically cracking up was always the challenge. We had a good laugh about our lack of musical talent.

We performed as a New Orleans-style ragtime band, with Darren on cornet, Charles on trombone, Glenn on electric guitar, and me on a single snare drum. We'd bought our instruments used at local garage sales or rented them for the school band. We played "When the Saints Go Marching In" and "Won't You Come Home Bill Bailey."

Then I had to get them to read the scripts correctly. Darren and Charles never got through a rehearsal or a performance at the top of the living room staircase without cracking up at the wrong times. They were not actors by any measure and never took the shows as seriously as I did.

"Darren, stop giggling," I'd say for the fifth time during an impromptu rehearsal.

"You're messing up the rhythm of the song."

"It's not me; it's Charlie," he'd say, laughing uncontrollably. "And what's 'rhythm'?"

"We're never going to get this right unless you take

this seriously," I'd scold, trying to be a perfectionist but always falling short of it. Charles, though laughing as well, would then become defensive.

"You're lying," he'd say to Darren. "I'm not laughing. I had a cough."

"Yeah, right," deadpanned Glenn, rolling his eyes and definitely not laughing or smiling. "Let's do this and get it over with."

I would spend hours writing scripts or working out a song, and then the boys would shrug it off as folderol. What did they care? They didn't want to do it in the first place. For them, this wasn't about creating entertainment; it was a diversion from doing chores.

During the shows, in between scenes, Melody and Kim would run up the stairs and hold up a white sheet as a makeshift curtain, then run back down when we were ready to start the next bit. That curtain was often taken down too soon, revealing me scrambling to set up a makeshift prop or embarrassingly struggling to put on a pair of pants. We were making do despite having very little in the way of material things.

Although she allowed these shows to take place, Mrs. Nelson never participated or helped in any way. In fact, she'd sometimes get mad when I wanted to get everyone together to practice. She felt we had better things to do.

Nonetheless, that "holiday feeling" has stayed with us. We'll never know what it was about the holidays that brought out the best in Mrs. Nelson, when she was so mean to us during other times of the year, but they were special events we still cherish. It's empowering what a little bit of Christmas magic can do.

10

OUR "BEST" FRIENDS

Pets, specifically finches and canaries, cats, frogs, turtles, and dogs, were a rewarding part of the Nelson house and a welcome distraction. Glenn and I liked birds. Although they were technically in the house for all to enjoy, I was given a yellow canary one Easter while Glenn got small Zebra finches with gray bodies and colorful orange beaks. This brought a constant chirping to the house. My bird was kept in a separate cage from Glenn's finches, which quickly multiplied like rabbits. It seems like we had to get bigger and bigger cages every few months to accommodate the growing brood, until at one point, Glenn had about fifteen birds in a tall cage.

"Those birds are driving me crazy," Mrs. Nelson would

say, mostly joking.

"Maybe we should cook them for dinner."

"No!" Glenn would say, fearing she might be serious. You never really knew with Mrs. Nelson.

We ended up trading the finches for turtles at a local pet store. Those eventually multiplied as well, but no one would take the turtles, so we ended up releasing them in a nearby pond.

When I first came to the Nelsons' house in 1969, Gil Jr. had a mutt dog named Noah that didn't like anyone but him. The dog often growled his displeasure, and we knew to stay clear. They say dogs mimic their owners, and this proved to be the case with Noah. He somehow intuitively knew that I was different from the rest and wanted nothing to do with me.

Years later, after Gil moved out of the house and took Noah with him, Mr. and Mrs. Nelson decided to buy a new dog. They initially discussed getting an Afghan because one of Gilbert Sr.'s coworkers bred them, but eventually settled on a beautiful St. Bernard puppy. We named him "Happy," because that's the way he made us feel. Another female St. Bernard followed about a year later. She was named "Chrissie," for Gerry's girlfriend at the time.

Chrissie soon joined Happy in the yard and lounging on the kitchen's aging linoleum floor. She was a sickly dog from the day we got her and died after about eighteen months, so a third St. Bernard arrived and we named her "Melody." This was done to appease our own Melody, who along with her brother, Glenn, was away at her mother's home in Florida at the time.

When Melody returned, she took one look at the dog and said, "This dog is ugly." Mrs. Nelson was not pleased, because she had only paid for the dog to make Melody feel welcome.

"Is that how you thank us for getting you a dog?" she grumbled, even though it was not really gotten for Melody alone. "Don't be ungrateful," Mrs. Nelson admonished.

After about three years, Melody the dog became ill. I drove in a car with Mr. Nelson to the veterinarian as she was hemorrhaging blood in large, coagulated pieces that we thought looked like pieces of a calf's liver. During the ride, while resting her head on my lap, she let out a huge sigh and died...right then and there. I was never very attached to her, but, without letting anyone see, I cried that night.

So, dogs didn't last very long in the Nelson household. Charles recalls the spring morning about ten years later when Mrs. Nelson roused him and Darren early one morning from a sound sleep. In the year leading up to this, Happy was not moving as well as he used to.

"The dog died; you have to go bury it in the yard."

She didn't bother to say, "Good morning."

So before going to school that day, Charles and Darren retrieved Happy from the cold bathroom floor where he'd expired, wrapped him in a blanket, and dragged him out of the house and into a wheelbarrow, as Mrs. Nelson instructed them to do.

They buried him under a small tree in the backyard. It was a sad day, according to Charles, and yet another chore he did not want but was expected to do. He remembers it this way:

My heart was deeply saddened. This dog that had given me (and others in the household) so many years of joy had suddenly passed away. And, if that wasn't bad enough, we were forced to bury him before we went to school! I know that Darren was feeling the same emotions I was. How could we bury this dog? There was something so wrong about it. But, like any other chore in the household, we did what we were told. No questions asked. So, we proceeded to put Happy in a cover that had a zipper that went all the way around it. I believe it was a sofa cover of some sort. And strangely enough, it was an ugly orange color. There was a horrible stench of death in the air.

We then carried Happy outside to the wheelbarrow, got two shovels and wheeled him to the backyard. We decided to bury him next to the pear tree. I clearly remember this because there was a huge rock next to the tree. Maybe we picked that spot because the stone was kind of a grave marker. We both dug the hole and put Happy in his final resting place. My whole body felt numb throughout the whole experience. And my heart was sad. As I'm sure Darren's was, too.

Darren has said he remembers the incident differently: it didn't leave a lasting effect on him at all.

"It was nothing, I took a shovel and buried the dog," he recalls, without blinking an eye. He also hinted that he did most of the work. "Then I went to school and that was the end of Happy."

I had left the Nelsons by this point, so I got the news of Happy's passing over the phone from Mrs. Nelson.

"Yep, she's gone," she said, almost matter-of-factly with a bit of guilt added because I wasn't around to help do something about it. "Don't dwell on things you have nothing to do with," she said, which I took as harsh but sound words of wisdom.

She knew we all loved that dog, despite his loud bellowing bark and constant slobbering that would get all over your hands, clothes and any surrounding hard surfaces when he shook his head. And there were always pieces of dog hair that seemed to be everywhere. But we'd spent hours together, alone, while I weeded the vegetable gardens or cleaned the garage. He always had her tongue hanging to the side, heavily panting and inevitably with some slobber dripping down.

Fun together also included bath time. It usually took three of us to bathe the dogs in a bathtub or outside with the garden hose. When we finished, the dog would shake his whole body and everything around for some distance got soaked along with him. I always had to change into dry clothes afterwards.

A mystery continues about who took the Easter ham from the kitchen counter when we were young. One minute it was cooling in a large platter as we prepared the table and the next it was gone. Happy was later found digging in the backyard. It may have been the best meal of his life.

Of all the pets we had, Happy was the favorite and was responsible for many good memories that to this day are joyfully invoked by us all.

11

HOW YA KEEP 'EM DOWN ON THE FARM

Just as suddenly as many of the other projects that came to be at the Nelson's, Mr. Nelson decided to stake our future, literally, on a heavily wooded forest in a remote farm town called Parkman, Maine. For two years beginning in 1974, he was enthralled with the idea of "living off the land" and other unconventional DIY notions garnered from stories he read in his beloved *Mother Earth News* and *Popular Mechanics* magazines and in books like "Walden" by Henry David Thoreau. Now he was envisioning his own Shangri-La.

The plot was a farm in theory only at that point, just raw land that needed a lot of manual labor to be fully realized. But he had his utopia and was off and running. You could see the excited lilt in in his step. As usual, Mr. Nelson assumed his word was the law and in this case, that meant we were moving.

The vision, as it was explained, was to build a house and a barn with lots of farm animals and a great big vegetable garden. In his mind, we wouldn't need to go to the grocery store often, perhaps ever. In actuality, it would be run like a commune.

The problem was that feelings, loyalties and people in the house were changing. We were all getting older, outsiders were infiltrating, and Mr. Nelson's word was becoming less a law and more an opinion that could be challenged. And some of the older kids had no interest in working on a farm.

Andy's wife Barbara, never a particular favorite of Mrs. Nelson's, remembers sitting at the kitchen table in Huntington with Gerry's current girlfriend, Cindy, when the land purchase was announced and discussing how crazy they thought the idea was.

"We both looked at each other and said, 'I wouldn't be caught dead on that farm,'" Barbara told me—and she said they meant it at the time. Well, if Cindy wasn't going, then Gerry wasn't either. Andy and Gil Jr. lived out of the house by then, so they were not realistic candidates for the pseudo-labor camp. What's more, Rose Ann, away at college, had no intention of wearing overalls and getting dirt under her fingernails. Andy and Melody were balking at the idea as well.

There was a crack in the Nelsons' dam, and it was leaking profusely.

Despite the family friction, Mr. Nelson forged on with

his ambitious idea and purchased one hundred and forty-seven acres of heavily wooded land for $100 per acre ($14,700 total) in the spring of 1975. The long-term plan now being set into motion included relocating the family after Kim, Melody, Glenn, and I graduated high school in three years (1978). Charles and Darren would be swept up in the farm as well, although their opinion, if they had one, was not even considered.

We began to ask questions amongst ourselves, which had rarely occurred due to our fear of retribution. An instinctive doubt began to creep in. Was this just another one of Mr. Nelson's crazy ideas, like the converted school bus, or the boat, or the methane gas generator: full of possibilities but useless in the end, now sitting in the yard unattended to?

With all of his prior ideas, each one of us kids had rallied around them, worked hard to make them happen, and then when Mr. Nelson lost interest, we moved on to the next project. It was clear Mr. Nelson needed us once again if his farm dream was going to come to fruition. Mrs. Nelson took care of that. She called us all together into the kitchen—actually Melody yelled for us to come "Now!"—and told us that this was a family endeavor and as such, we all had to commit to and subsidize it. It was our "duty."

So, the raw acreage on which this Catholic kibbutz would be built was partially purchased with money supplied by Kim, Glenn, and I, who had all shown interest in the farm. The money came out of our savings accounts, earned from various part-time summer jobs. We didn't really have a choice; we were simply told to fork it over, and we did.

"Mike, you've got money in your bank account," Mrs.

Nelson said in front of the other kids. This was money I had planned to use for college, but she had one thing on her mind: funding the farm.

"I'll drive with you to the bank to withdraw it," she offered. "Who else is going to contribute?" It was like a come-to-Jesus fundraising event in our kitchen.

Without hesitation, I emptied my account of $3,000. Glenn and Kim were also urged to surrender funds and each gave similar amounts. It was everything we had to our names. Glenn was so pissed at the time, but under the influence of a heavy amount of guilt, mixed with the Nelsons' sense of entitlement to us and everything we owned, he feebly surrendered. We all did.

As there were no buildings or pre-built structures on the Parkman land, Mr. Nelson bought a single-wide mobile home that would serve as a base camp and had it moved onto the property. That trailer was paid for with more of our money. For us foster kids, resistance was futile.

Gil Jr. and Gerry were not at that family meeting and never offered up a dime. They weren't even factored into the whole farm equation. Without saying it out loud, the parents gave them a choice not to go and they took it. They were young adults by now and enjoyed an independence that wasn't afforded to the rest of us kids. We didn't have the courage to voice discontent. They just said "No."

That's why, one hot day in the summer of 1976, Glenn and I found ourselves tramping the boundaries of the expansive and only partially cleared land. We were all alone, deep in the woods, as Mr. Nelson had gone into town to finish up some paperwork for the purchase of the property. It was spooky and exhilarating at the same time. Glenn scared easily in those days.

He and I walked along a barely used path with many old and decaying rock walls. We were seeing the land for the first time and cataloging the different types of trees on the property, per Mr. Nelson's orders. There were massive elms, birches, oaks, pines, and an assortment of others I had never seen before. I broke off a leaf from each type of tree, as specifically instructed by Mr. Nelson, and placed it inside a notebook to let it dry and flatten out. Later, I would look it up in a book called "The Trees of Maine."

"Learn the leaves," Mr. Nelson commanded, taking a cue from the Native American Indians he idolized, "and you'll know a lot about the ground you are standing on."

We even crossed paths with a large female moose, which initially scared the hell out of Glenn and me, being suburban Long Islanders.

"What's that?" Glenn said, in a panicked voice.

"It's a moose," I said, getting a better first look.

"That's not a moose," said Glenn.

"It looks like a moose," I said.

"It doesn't have antlers," said Glenn.

He was right, which made me wonder how tough the creature really was. No antlers meant it was a female moose. We began jumping up and down and making loud noises to scare it away, which turned out to be a bad idea. The animal charged at us for about four seconds, long enough to make us run in the opposite direction as fast as we could until we grew tired of running. Mr. Nelson did not witness this scene and didn't seem to believe us when we told him about it later.

But Glenn and I laughed out loud about it, accusing each other of being cowards in the face of danger. We were cowards, but there was never any real danger. The moose was yards away from us at all times.

"Chicken!" we both said, almost simultaneously, and laughed again.

***

While some of the older kids didn't want anything to do with the farm, I was fascinated by the idea of moving to Maine because as a young kid in Queens, I had always longed for wide open spaces. In addition, and perhaps more importantly, I saw this as a viable idea that Mr. Nelson and I truly shared. Cataloging the leaves from the trees on the Maine property was the first real father-son interaction we ever had that wasn't linked to a menial task around the house. Surveying the property was incredibly interesting, like a scientific mission...albeit with lots of mosquitoes. As he had done in Huntington, Mr. Nelson was intent on designing and building the home himself— with no outside help, only us kids. The task was to identify the types of trees available for the future house: hardwoods like birch and oak were good for flooring; pine and elm would make good siding.

Glenn and I were both sixteen years old and enjoying the adventure of it all. The idea of moving up north was so far out that it was exciting beyond belief. We spent an entire week up there getting it all done, and about a month later Mr. Nelson finalized the purchase of the property. We soon had a well drilled and a septic tank installed, paid for with money from Kim and Glenn ($1,500 each).

Unfortunately, or perhaps not, the naysayers won out in the end and no one ever moved up to that farm. Although Mr. Nelson continued to pay taxes on the property, the ensuing years saw it lie in ruin, much like the school bus and the boat. The trailer on the property was broken into several times, with vandals leaving behind beer cans, spent cigarettes and drug paraphernalia. In the end, we all came to the conclusion that living on a farm required much more effort than learning to weld a pipe or putting a new roof on a house. This would be a lifestyle change—one, ultimately, we all weren't prepared to make.

12

SEXUAL AWAKENING

As four of us grew into adolescence at the same exact time, a more palpable type of tension began to permeate the house: sexual tension. Now all seventeen years old, Kim, Melody, Glenn, and I were all in the throes of teenage awareness, and our hormones were raging. I discovered the wonders of masturbation via an old, grainy black-and-white (8mm) silent porn film in Gerry's room. With a friend from school, I had gotten into making short horror films and editing them on a small viewer/editor, cutting the film with a razor blade and splicing the scenes together with Scotch tape. So, I knew a bit about watching black and white film on reels.

I would sneak upstairs to Gerry's room to get the film canister, take it and my small hand-cranked reel-to-reel viewer down to the basement, and do my thing. When I was finished, I would hurriedly run upstairs to put the movie back. One time, Gerry nearly caught me, but I wasn't deterred. I repeated this transgression about twenty times.

The Nelsons were clearly aware of my awakening sexuality because they brought it to the attention of a doctor at the Angel Guardian Agency in April 1977. A caseworker wrote this about me in his file:

Adjustment reaction to adolescence, struggling with strong dependency yearnings. Conflicts focus on relationship with maternal figure. Conflicts around self-image and personal adequacy. Mrs. Nelson concerned with his excessive masturbation.

Homosexuality was her prime concern. Husband does not see this.

I was prescribed some pills to make me sleep at night and told by the agency doctor to "play a lot of sports to get rid of that energy."

It turns out I wasn't the only one acting on these new feelings. Gil Jr. had taken more than a passing liking to Kim, and secretly the two began an intimate relationship. They were not siblings by blood, so it might be considered okay by some, but when I found out, it was life-altering for me—but not for the obvious reasons. Despite my new-found lust, I never pictured any of us together like that. I was on my bed reading when I heard noises coming from Mr. and Mrs. Nelson's bedroom. I walked in on Kim and Gil Jr. in the throes of passion. Kim was seventeen, and Gil Jr. was 26. They looked at me but didn't move. I was more surprised than they were and ran out, envisioning an ensuing beating from Gil Jr.

But it didn't come. I anxiously waited a day, then two, but not a word was spoken about it by anyone. The suspense was killing me. Then, sure enough, about a week later, while I was cleaning up the garage yet again, Gil Jr. came up behind me and held a .22-caliber Ruger pistol—a replica German Luger—to my head. He said he had been waiting to see if I would say anything to Mr. or Mrs. Nelson, and I hadn't.

"If you ever tell anyone, I will kill you," was his simple yet direct statement. It was the first time since I had left St. Michael's that I truly felt scared for my life. I flashed back to those long, intimidating days and nights in the orphanage and heard a *click* of the bullet being engaged in the chamber. The gun was loaded.

Terrified, I mumbled that I wouldn't say anything, ever. The intimidating secret ate me up inside, so after about two weeks, I decided to tell Mrs. Nelson. She always welcomed information on someone else in the house and I saw this as a chance to get in her good graces. Mrs. Nelson always cut our hair at home, literally bowl-style, at the dining room table. She was cutting my hair when I told her—perhaps not the best timing. I described what I had seen, and, caught off guard, she nervously clipped my ear with the scissors. She said she would "get to the bottom of it."

I can't explain why—maybe it was my bloody ear—but as my words came out, I got the impression she already knew about Kim and Gil Jr. We never spoke about it again, and I felt stupid for mentioning it. There were no brownie points to be had this time.

Kim and Gil Jr. continued to sneak out at night and carry on in the house, albeit out of sight of the Nelson parents. About six months later, I overheard Mrs. Nelson talking with someone about Gil Jr. and Kim, in a sort of guilt-free explanatory way.

"It will work itself out," she said.

I realized then that Mrs. Nelson did indeed know about Kim and Gil Jr. and she did nothing to stop it...in her own house.

***

By the summer of 1977 the winds of change were blowing forcefully. For me, to my surprise, they felt good. But there were still rules that had to be followed and unwanted situations that had to be navigated.

Gil Jr. moved out of the house and the Nelsons relocated Gerry into the room Glenn, Charles, Darren, and I had previously shared upstairs, next to Kim and Melody's room. Gerry wanted his own space and he got it. We four (Glenn and I at age twelve, and Charles and Darren at age eight) were moved into the smallest bedroom—right next to Mr. and Mrs. Nelson's.

The room was barely big enough for a bunk bed and a trundle bed, but that's where the four of us slept; two on the bunk bed and the other two on the trundle. We weren't given a choice. The room also had an attic staircase that pulled down from the ceiling. The roof was in need of repair and you could hear the wind whistling through the wood seams on a blustery day. Sometimes we'd go up there to hang out at night when the Nelsons weren't paying attention, but in the summer, it was hot and so full of boxes that there wasn't a lot of open space.

Gerry now had the larger room all to himself. This enabled him to get into all kinds of mischief without being seen, and he took full advantage. He had shady friends—some we recognized, others we didn't—coming and going out of his room, and he lived there with his girlfriend Cindy for a while. This led to an unpredictable situation that was a bad influence on everyone.

Increasingly, he was not doing anything to hide his misconduct, and Mrs. Nelson, despite her "good Catholic" ways, reluctantly allowed this to occur. Glenn and I always thought his total freedom was a bit unfair and began to express this to her. She grew increasingly agitated every time we told her of another misdeed we'd seen (or smelled). She said she wasn't listening to our "nonsense" and never offered any justifiable reasons for his mis-behavior. Cindy's presence was a natural progression of Gerry's maturity, at least that's what we were told.

"It's nice the way they are together," she would say, disingenuously, while Gerry and Cindy screamed at each other in the background. Theirs was a rocky coupling at best.

Even while she looked the other way, there was no denying that Mrs. Nelson was losing control of her own household, a place she had always ruled. So, she tightened her grip. None of kids would be allowed the same cohabitation privileges. I had a girlfriend at seventeen but was told not to bring her around the house. I wasn't allowed to use the car either, so dating was a challenge, better left to my visiting her exclusively.

About a year later, Gerry and Cindy moved out and got their own apartment. We got our larger room back, which made us very happy. But it was short-lived. Gerry and Cindy lasted about two years and then he returned to live in the Nelsons' house. So back we moved—Glenn, Charles, Darren, and me—into the smallest bedroom in the house. It wasn't ideal, we all agreed, but at least we were rooming together. That gave us some solace. And there were those slipper fights to look forward to. They never happened in the larger room.

***

With uncertainty swirling, the Nelsons' house had become a powder keg of pent up, yet always unspoken, feelings that were bound to explode. We were now getting older, more aware of our surroundings and looking for clues to where we fit in the world at large. We began to shun about busy-work projects and increasingly used school work as an excuse to be lazy. Our friends at school were also beginning to have an influence on us, and that was not good news for the parents. Like a rite of passage, Kim, Melody, Glenn and I were all the same pubescent age and began to think we knew better. To Mrs. Nelson, there was nothing worse than a foster kid with an attitude problem. She had four of them emotionally raging at once.

Mrs. Nelson herself was also changing. She had been very religious when we were growing up, but one day without any advance notice or explanation, we stopped going to church. I woke up one Sunday morning to find that we were instead clipping the hedges on the side of the property. This meant a lot of sweat and the fear of getting stung by a bee. The hedges were notoriously good at concealing hornet's nests, until it was too late.

"No church today," Mrs. Nelson said when we came down to the kitchen table for breakfast. She had the power to change our world that way. I think we were relieved to skip church, until... "There's too much to do around here. It's not going to get done itself."

With no church, Mrs. Nelson became increasingly erratic and would fly off the handle at the slightest provocation. There had been a time when she wouldn't have dreamed of using a swear word (and would stick a bar of soap in our mouths if *we* did), but now she was prone to foulmouthed rants.

There were mornings when we'd wake up to the sound of her cursing like a trucker in the kitchen. At the time, I wrote a short story for school entitled "My Mother the Truck Driver," about a woman who "FU'd" her way through life and said nasty things that upset everyone. Sometimes fiction comes from truth; in this case, it certainly did. I got an A+ from the teacher, who asked me to read my composition aloud in class.

We kids weren't sure what to make of Mrs. Nelson's new confrontational persona, and I certainly didn't dare tell her about my school assignment.

So, religion was out and our weekly car rides together ended because the Nelsons said so. Period. It's ironic that during all the years of going to Mass on Sunday, Mrs. Nelson spent considerable effort (and money) dressing up all of us kids in semi-matching attire—sport jackets for the boys, and dresses, hats, and gloves for the girls. She'd lay out the clothes on the living room couch, one outfit after another, early in the morning before we woke up.

"And boys, don't try to put your hands in the pockets of your jackets, I sewed them shut," were her instructions.

THE BOND

She stitched together our jacket pockets until Glenn and I were well into our teens.

13

EASING THE PAIN

Gerry's return to the Nelsons' home after breaking up with Cindy heralded an era of drinking, drugs, and robbery. He was now openly rebelling against not only his parents but everyone and everything around him. He barked at us kids whenever he got the chance and he was doing badly in school. The red flags were everywhere and really were impossible not to see, but no adults intervened. At age twenty, he wanted nothing to do with us kids and was given carte blanche to come and go as he pleased. Gerry even had his own section in the refrigerator, while we foster kids were not allowed to even open it without permission.

I was now eighteen and also experimenting with alcohol and hanging out more with friends from high school. Mostly, I was trying to stay away from the house. I found refuge in beer's ability to help me forget my circumstances. I didn't like who I was, yet I was scared to death of making a change.

Without knowing any of the details, my friends got me through a lot of hard times; even if our choices were not the healthiest. Sometimes we'd drive to a cornfield, drink cheap wine (Annie Green Springs), and sing and play guitar—mostly songs by the Eagles, Genesis, and the Beatles. We thought we sounded pretty good, but there's a good chance it sounded like two dogs howling at the moon, one in pain.

I was yelled at for staying out past nine o'clock on a Saturday night, while huge wafts of pot smoke emanated from Gerry's room and no one said anything about it. He was also growing marijuana plants in his room (and in the backyard garden), and everyone in the house knew it. Yet, Mr. and Mrs. Nelson figuratively (and, I'm guessing, literally) held their noses and looked the other way. Maybe the guilt of the burden she had brought upon her own children was beginning to weigh on Mrs. Nelson. When it came to her own son, she could no longer distinguish between right and wrong.

A rash of "new" objects, like an expensive bicycle, lawnmowers and a stereo, began showing up in the garage. There was no mystery about who was responsible. I hesitated to say anything at first but finally did, and Mr. Nelson told me to ignore them. The Nelsons had to know these items were stolen property, but they didn't want to admit it or, say anything about it. They had grown afraid of Gerry and what he had become.

Another time, one of Gerry's friends from the neighborhood stole my bicycle, a chrome silver-framed ten-speed Schwinn that I bought at a garage sale with my own money. I used it to get to and from my summer job. I loved that bike. I modified it with a special bracket on the back that I fashioned out of sheet metal and used to pull things in a cart. For a few weeks, I was very proud of my engineering prowess. Then suddenly the bike was gone. When I found out who took it, I was furious and told Mrs. Nelson so. She sided with the thief.

"It's your own fault, you shouldn't have left it in the driveway unattended," she said, defending Gerry's friend, but really Gerry.

"But I know who took it," I implored.

"Just let it go," she responded, and that was the end of it. Gerry was left unscathed and I never got another bicycle. I had to walk or hitch rides for most of that summer. It was a frustrating time.

***

And yet, Mrs. Nelson remained very protective of our image as a family (as she was of her own) and cared deeply about how the outside world saw us kids. She resented that the term "foster child" carried a stigma. Kim had an issue with another kid at school calling her "dirt" because she had three foster siblings in the same grade. Mrs. Nelson jumped to her defense and demanded a meeting with the principal. The meeting lasted about an hour and ended with a terse admonition from the principal to the kid who disrespected Kim.

"Don't call them foster kids," he said. It seemed he got the message too.

Mrs. Nelson put up a fight to save our honor. At least, that's what she told us on many occasions, often during a speech about the importance of family.

"You are a family," she'd bark, military style. "Act like it. The world is not going to help you; you have to help yourselves. I'm not going to do it."

That meant sticking up for each other at school and putting on a united front in public, even though in front of our friends—and we all had different ones—we were a bit embarrassed by the attention it brought. It wasn't normal that four kids from one family were the same age and in the same grade, but we were. Even to us, as we grew older, it felt a bit strange.

However, we all came to believe her one-for-all-and-all-for-one creed, because that's exactly what we wanted to hear. Our hearts swelled and we wore that comradery with pride.

14

OUR EXODUS

In the summer of 1977, I sat with my small General Electric solid-state AM-band transistor radio glued to my ear, listening late into the night to funny parody songs on *The Dr. Demento Show* and to 1010 WINS (*"You give us twenty-two minutes, we'll give you the world."*) for the latest news on the "Son of Sam" killer. I began spending more and more time with friends, which drove Mrs. Nelson to emotionally segregate me from the other kids. She always felt that we should be—we should want to be—at home working on the house or garden and not cavorting with our peers. It was our duty to the family, she'd say, that should always come first.

While I had played sports in junior high school—wrestling, soccer, and football—now that I was in high school, I tried out but was forced to quit each team due to the guilt imposed on me. When I came home from a practice or a game at the beginning of a season, Mrs. Nelson would look at me with disapproval, and that was that. She had that kind of power over me and I didn't want to disappoint her.

"Do you think it's fair that everyone else comes home straight after school but you?" she'd ask, after I'd tried out for a week and made the team. "It's one thing to play sports but another to neglect your chores at home. I'm not making up your mind for you." She could really lay on the guilt. "You should know the right thing to do."

And so, one day I was one of the best players on the soccer team or one of the fastest sprinters on the track-and-field team, and the next day I'd quit. I'd have to sheepishly walk into my coach's office and make up an injury as a reason for leaving the team when the last thing I wanted to do was quit. It was frustrating having to lie to avoid telling the truth about Mrs. Nelson's desire to keep me home, working on the house. To this day I can still feel the frustration and embarrassment of it.

I also performed in the school plays and was a member of the video production club, but Mr. and Mrs. Nelson never came to a single performance or saw a single (black-and-white) video I produced. At this point, I realized I was becoming a persona non grata and I could feel the burden of that, but I couldn't do anything to stop it. The emotional distance between us had now grown to the size of the Grand Canyon. I was losing my place in the Nelson household, and the feeling was profound...and disastrous.

I was being squeezed between a rock and a hard place. The stifling undercurrent of toxicity and the fear of not knowing what to expect from the Nelsons became like living with a disgruntled spouse while waiting for a divorce to become final. It reached the point where neither the Nelsons nor I wanted to be in the same room together. In their minds, I was going to college against their wishes and thus had to be removed. It was the only leverage they had over me left. I could feel it in the way they spoke to me and how I was now literally excluded from family conversations. I'd walk into a room, and they would stop talking. It was also in their body language.

"Oh, don't worry, we're not talking about you," they'd lie, shooing me away.

"There's nothing for you here. Why don't you go do something, like straighten up the garage?"

My fury was mounting with every interaction. One day my friend, Kevin, unexpectedly came to the house to visit. I was happy to see him, innocently forgetting the "no friends in the house" policy that only applied to me. As we talked in the kitchen, Kevin casually jumped up and sat on the counter, which was about waist high. None of us had ever dared do that; it was forbidden but Kevin couldn't have known. I froze for a second as Mr. Nelson walked past and motioned to me to get Kevin off. Sensing the tension, Kevin and I left the room and went outside.

Kevin asked if I was okay. I said, "Sure." What else could I say? Kevin got in his car and left. I felt relief that Mr. Nelson didn't make a scene in front of my best friend. That, too, had happened before.

I came back into the house to find Mr. Nelson standing in the kitchen doorway waiting for me, with hands on hips and his face fuming.

"Why would you allow that kid to sit on the counter?"

he asked rhetorically.

This was a surface that was covered in old and very worn linoleum.

"Is this counter a chair? Or that one?" He pointed irately to the right side of the kitchen sink and then the left side for dramatic emphasis.

When I didn't provide a satisfactory answer, or any answer, he hauled off and punched me squarely on the right side of my face. It caught me completely off guard. I dropped to the ground then quickly got up. My boxing training at the orphanage was being put to the test.

When you get knocked down, get up or risk looking "soft."

"If you ever let that happen again, you will not be allowed in this house," Mr. Nelson barked at me. "And I don't want to see you right now, either! Go up to your room."

I was totally flabbergasted and in pain. I fought not to cry in front of him and saved my tears for later, tasting blood with each painful swallow.

As I walked upstairs, Mrs. Nelson said to me, "He shouldn't have hit you, but you deserved that. This house is not a playground for your friends."

Then came the typical Mrs. Nelson reprimand to whatever I was doing "wrong" around the house, like sitting on the couch with my shoes on. "Do you know how much that counter cost?"

Most things with her came down to the cost of things. Including me.

***

January 20, 1978 was a particularly nerve-wracking eighteenth birthday day for me, as it meant that I, like thousands of young adults coming up through the foster care system before me, had "aged out" of the system. The state was no longer legally responsible for my upbringing, and it was time for me to go. I knew this to be true and yet hoped that the Nelsons would look past that inevitable milestone and deem me worthy of adoption. They could be my forever family.

Getting older is not something you can avoid or protect against. Biological offspring will tell you they can't grow up fast enough. Foster kids don't have that luxury. You know that birthday is coming but are helpless to do anything to slow life down. To a foster care child with nowhere to go, it's like you become day-old bread that no one wants to touch with a ten-foot pole. It's a dreaded day. And even though I sensed my time at the Nelsons' was coming to a close a year before that, I still didn't want to leave. Where would I go?

***

Even with all the anxieties that came with growing older, I was still sold on the idea of moving to Maine and living on the farm with them. I reasoned that I could take the misery of it meant staying around. My insides were calling to somehow keep my place in the family. I thought the farm might make things better for our family as a whole. That's all I still really cared about. I just had to hold on tightly a bit longer, I reasoned, and figure out a way. I frantically looked everywhere, but there was nothing firm to grasp on to.

Indeed, like my ring in the orphanage, I refused to give in. My family was slipping away and I wasn't going to let to go easily. They say love is work but holding on to the Nelsons was hard labor. In May 1978, it was time to graduate from high school. Looking ahead, I only applied to colleges located in Maine, figuring that would keep me close to the farm. Mr. and Mrs. Nelson, however, were not supportive of my going to college at all. They expected me to forego my studies and just work on the farm.

"Where's the money coming from to go to college?" Mrs. Nelson asked, as I began the arduous application process. This was before the Internet.

What wasn't clear then, but is now, is that my inclination for farm life was not really born of my own desires. I was doing what I thought would make the Nelsons happy. They had taught me—and it was ingrained in my brain after nine years with them—to shelve my personal goals.

However, with things at home growing increasingly unhealthy and stressful, I knew that I needed a higher education. Besides, most of my high school friends were going away to college. Watching them get accepted to the schools of their choice, it seemed unnatural not to apply too. I was as smart as they were.

Although unsure of how to go about it, I was frantic to find a school that would accept me and give me a healthy financial aid check. I had no one to show me the process and I had put off applying until after graduation. Many of the larger schools were filled up at that point. I thought I had found a compromise when I applied and was accepted to Ricker College in Houlton, Maine. When I proudly showed Mrs. Nelson the letter of acceptance, she again said, "How are you planning to pay for this?" I had no idea, but I knew I wanted to go. Gil Jr. had gone through two years of college and then dropped out. My sister Rose Ann had gone to SUNY New Paltz, in upstate New York, but none of the other kids in the Nelson household had any ambition to attend college. They found work far more rewarding because there was no studying and you got paid real money, something we saw very little of growing up. The sirens' lure of cash was there, but I resisted. I wanted to further myself.

***

So, I wanted to leave and go against the family, while simultaneously fighting the urge—and the Nelsons' de-sire—to stay forever. Furthering my education was not solely about finding a good-paying job, though. I somehow knew in my heart that if I didn't go to college, I would never get to see the places I'd always dreamed of seeing—like the Grand Canyon.

Then I received a letter from Ricker College announc-ing that it had filed for bankruptcy and was closing only a few months before I was supposed to start there in September. Luckily, the school's admissions staff took pity of me and helped me find another school: Franklin Pierce College (it's now a university), in Rindge, New Hampshire. Against Mrs. Nelson's "better judgment," I enrolled. The decision made me feel both excited at the prospect of moving on with my life, and tense, not knowing how I would pay the tuition or what my new role with the Nelsons would be.

In early July 1978, I met with my biological father in

New York City and we went to see the musical "Hello, Dolly!" He was no longer playing the piano at this point and was still drinking, although he seemed to be limiting his intake a bit. He was working as a clerk at a large insurance company in the city. Our conversation was coherent, if a bit stunted with the reality that he had put us on this road to misery.

My only focus was going to college. I had to get away. I asked him for tuition help, and he replied confidently, in between hacking smoker's coughs, "I'll see what I can do."

I never saw a dime.

***

Meanwhile, Gerry had become more hostile. The drugs were wreaking havoc on everyone. There were several incidents in which he bloodied Mr. Nelson's face in a fit of rage. During one such blow-up, they got into a heated argument while Gerry was (to use Glenn's description), "higher than a five-winged kite." He was so stoned that he had Mr. Nelson in a chokehold and was literally squeezing the life out of his own father. Glenn jumped on Gerry's back and started choking him, which in turn led to Gerry releasing his grip on Mr. Nelson to keep from passing out himself.

Gerry stood up, astonished that someone had fought back. He ran through the living room looking for something to destroy when he spied Glenn's finches. Gerry pulled one of the birds out of the cage, threw it on the floor, and stomped on it until it was squashed dead. Seeing this, Glenn angrily punched Gerry. Gerry ran out of the house and into the nearby woods, trying to smash the windshield of the family car in the driveway with a garden rake on his way. Luckily, the glass did not break.

After the ugly scene we all witnessed, Mrs. Nelson complimented Glenn for fighting back and asked me why I hadn't done anything. I felt rattled; I had been too frozen with fear to make a stand like Glenn did.

"A lot of help *you* were," she chided me. Mrs. Nelson had a point. I felt inadequate for not fighting Gerry.

To this day we're all certain Glenn's heroic actions saved Mr. Nelson's life. Glenn had a conversation with Gerry years later about the violent incident and Gerry, who is now sober, thanked him for jumping in. Gerry admitted that on that day, in his drug-fueled condition, he would have killed his father.

***

As I was preparing to leave Huntington for college, I got word from Mrs. Nelson that my father, Cosmo, had died the previous evening, ironically, on August 13th, 1978, the very same day he'd been born fifty-six years earlier. The cause was complications from cirrhosis of the liver. He drank himself to death while living alone in a small room in Richmond Hill, Queens. Besides asking for money for college, my last conversation with him touched on why we were abandoned.

"I can't understand why you sent us away," I said.

"You don't fully understand and I can't explain it," he replied, adding that he had done the right thing by giving us away. That was that.

The funeral was a military-style affair and there were very few people there. My sisters and brother were there, as were my grandmother and a few uncles and other relatives, but Mr. and Mrs. Nelson did not attend. Neither did any of the other foster kids. I rode in a black limo to Long Island National Cemetery and stood close to the graveside as the coffin was lowered into the ground. It was exactly like the thousands of military graves, all lined up in rows as far as the eye could see. It was in the same plot where my mother was buried in 1968.

A priest said a few words, and a soldier in formal uniform folded the flag that had been draped over the coffin into a tight triangle and handed it to me. I looked at the flag and realized this was now the remaining link I had to my natural father. It felt like an overly starched shirt, all stiff and perfectly folded into a triangular shape. After all the hardship and pain he had caused, Cosmo was now being lowered into a hole in the ground. I couldn't watch the cemetery crew shovel dirt on him. I looked away. The entire service lasted about twenty minutes, far less time than it took us to drive there.

My biological parents had never gotten along in life, now they're lying together forever in death. One two-sided headstone is all that remains.

As I rode home in the rented stretch limousine, I forced myself to cry because I could see that there was no sympathy among those gathered. I was the only person to shed a tear. Many who really knew him considered Cosmo a bad guy and a drunk, and their absence attested to that. I felt sad that all I had wanted to talk about when I saw him just a month before was figuring out how to get money for college. That request now seemed crass and pitiful.

I was told by an acquaintance at the funeral that

Cosmo had felt ashamed that he had put his children in an orphanage. He never told me anything like. He did say, many years after we were living in Huntington, that he found solace in the fact that Rose Ann, Charles, and I were not sent to different homes.

"I kept you together," he said, but that wasn't justify-cation for us.

He never saw the reality that we saw: that our family was in pieces and he was the perpetrator. It was he who had thrown us away. I was told by my grandmother to stop trying to understand why it happened the way it did, but I've never stopped trying to reconcile it.

Although I hadn't lived with him for ten years by that point, and he never showed an interest in bringing me to live with him, I was overcome with a sense of nostalgia for my young childhood and the father I never got to know well. The spooky phrase "life without father..." mystically crept into my head and stayed with me for days. Sometimes you long for things you never had and add a certain romanticism to fill in the voids. I think I did that with my father, despite his flaws and abandonment. Everybody needs a father, right?

When I returned to Huntington that evening, after a long exhausting day, Mr. Nelson was far from nurturing. As I walked around depressed for the next few days, he callously invoked his favorite put-down, more than once, "What's wrong with you?" He clearly knew the answer but failed to see the full picture. Or didn't care enough to offer support. I wanted to yell at him that my father had just died, but I could never muster the courage to respond to him that way. Taking the path of least resistance with Mr. Nelson kept us out of his crosshairs of discontent.

Keep your head down.

***

About a week after the funeral and a few weeks before I was to leave for college, I decided to end my life, right then and there. I didn't want to be at the Nelsons' house anymore and in my mind, I had run out of options. I had had enough of being sad and I really believed it was the only sensible way out. I had stolen a bottle of Valium from the desk of the principal of the local junior high school where I worked during the summers since I was thirteen. My job entailed eight hours a day of scraping gum off the bottom of desks and painting over the scribbles and profane language on classroom walls.

I was sitting in the backyard with a bottle of beer and my acoustic guitar (as I had been doing increasingly to pass the time, make sense of my emotions, and steer clear of confrontation). That night a song came to me in a haunting Middle Eastern style. Influenced by the voice in my head, the lyrics came out more like a personal plea for sympathy. This was not planned.

Life without father is no fun.
I once had a father, but now he's gone. He left me.
He left me.
I'm so alone.
Life was fun when he was here,
But now he's gone and things seem so unclear. Life without
father is no fun. On, pretty momma, I'm on the run.
He left me.
He left me. I'm so alone.

As I drank the beer, I began to take the pills...first one, then another, and another. I was done with carrying the weight of the entire world on my shoulders. Taking pills was easy. Then, just as I was about to take yet another, my friend Kevin unexpectedly pulled up in his car. The universe had miraculously intervened. Sensing my condition, Kevin convinced me to ride with him. So, we drove around for a few hours and then he brought me home and I fell asleep on the front lawn. I woke up around four in the morning and snuck back inside the house and into my bed. Mr. and Mrs. Nelson did not know I had been out all night. I certainly did not volunteer anything about my almost-disastrous solution to my problems. My cry for help went unnoticed, but I was glad it had—and that Kevin had stopped me from my stupidity.

"Don't be a martyr" is what Mrs. Nelson would have said, had she known. She had given me this advice many times before when I expressed discontent about some injustice in my life. Hers was not a shoulder to cry on.

As the Nelsons had trained me, I survived my father's passing and just moved on. I figured it out.

When it was time to leave for college, I didn't have a ride. The Nelsons did not volunteer to drive me; they told me I had to find my own way. So, with two old suitcases packed with everything I owned, I began to walk out the door, anticipating a four-hour bus trip from Huntington to New Hampshire. As the taxi, which I had called for myself, arrived to pick me up, Mrs. Nelson suddenly appeared. It was afternoon and Mr. Nelson and the other kids weren't around.

It was a bit sad that there was no one to see me off

except the one person I was happy to be moving away from in the first place. She was clearly not sorry to see me go. Before I left, she made me open my two suitcases (which I had salvaged from the side of the road during one of our "Junk Day" excursions) and she rummaged through my neatly packed clothes to see if I was taking anything valuable from the house. I didn't have a thing of hers and being made to open my suitcases like a criminal at a border crossing was humiliating.

In the end, despite everything, leaving the Nelson household was one of the hardest things I've ever done. Sadly, throughout my entire ordeal in Huntington, I naïvely never understood the situation for what it really was: at eighteen, once the state-funded support payments were gone, so was I.

***

At Franklin Pierce College, I found a new freedom as well as an aspect of life that scared the hell out of me: choice. At college, I had to decide what food I ate and what clothes I wore. It was all new to me and I was hesitant at first. There was no more "we" or us." It was just me, trying to figure out who I was as an individual. In the Nelsons' house, you were told what to do and you did it. There was no lengthy thought process about what a particular shoe looked like on you. I was given a pair of shoes that just so happened to the exact same shoes as Glenn got. The Nelsons always bought in bulk, or else we got clothes worn by Gerry and Gil Jr. a year or two earlier. Throughout junior high school, I remember wearing a pair of shoes with a small tear in the side that had been Gerry's.

Now it was up to me to sink or swim, and I relished the autonomy.

I felt emboldened knowing that other people were interacting with me, liking what they saw. And I had a say in how they saw me. I became more confident as the school year wore on—joining the soccer team and the drama club and was voted freshman class president by a wide margin. A very likeable personality began to emerge, and my life outside of the Nelson house was feeling pretty good.

Then the Christmas holiday rolled around and I was faced with a decision I was nervous to confront ever since I had left the house. While everyone else around me was arranging to be picked up by their parents or catching rides with other students to their respective homes, I had nowhere to go and the college was closing the dorms for a two-week break. I called my sister Rose Ann and stayed with her family in New Paltz, New York. She was now married and had two small children of her own, Bartholomew and Hollyann.

When the end of the school year came in May, I faced the same dilemma. Where should I go? This time I got nostalgic and called Mrs. Nelson. That familial pull was still there, even if I didn't admit it outwardly. Bracing for the worst, I nervously huddled in an outside phone booth on campus and called her to ask if I could stay at their house for the summer. She answered curtly that I could stay with them for the summer if I got a job and paid $25 per week rent.

I was taken aback that she would charge me rent but looking to avoid the embarrassment of being the only student on my dorm floor that didn't have a home, I agreed. That summer was spent mostly avoiding each other, both inside and outside the house, and I returned to college in the fall unscathed. I had a good-paying job as a janitor at the junior high school, but by August I was eager to get back to school and my new family of friends.

***

When it was time to go back to college for my sophomore year. I was once again faced with having to take a bus to school. I was angrily packing my two old suitcases when Glenn offered to give me a ride in his beat-up 1964 Ford Falcon, with its antiquated three-gear stick shift on the steering column (Glenn called it "three on the tree").

The problem was, the car was falling apart and wouldn't make the four-hour trip due to a broken gear. But Glenn was offering, so he and I blindly took on the challenge of repairing it. We got a Chilton's Auto Repair manual and spent many hours and much trial and error (mostly error) literally taking apart that fifteen-year-old manual transmission and putting it back together on our own. Mr. Nelson, who was well versed in auto repair, adamantly left us to figure it out. It took us three days, but we did it.

Our only oversight was that we had three or four bolts left when we were finished, and never figured out where they went.

"Um, aren't we supposed to use all of these?" I asked Glenn, holding them in my hand.

"Oops," Glenn replied, and we both had a good laugh. "We'll see what happens on the road."

Glenn and I drove the four hours to my school in New

Hampshire and the car's transmission worked like a top. I'll never forget Glenn's generosity and our joint—and not always fun— astuteness in figuring out how to fix that car. Thus, we added "car mechanic" to the long list of things we learned by doing (along with welding, carpentry, gardening, roofing, etc.) and felt good about ourselves. We basked in the knowledge that we did it together, without Mr. Nelson's help. In fact, there was never an acknowledgment of our mechanical feat from him. We were learning to take matters into our own hands.

***

While away at college, I was always eager to get the gossip about life back at the Nelsons', which came in dribs and drabs from random phone conversations I had with the other kids. I learned Kim had begun to grow tired of Gil Jr. and began dating other guys. One, named Andy, allegedly had connections to the local Long Island mob. At least that's the story that's circulated around the family. This Andy drove a brand-new, rather ostentatious red Cadillac convertible. According to family gossip (although, again, I was out of the house at the time), Gil Jr. and Andy got involved in an argument, fueled by Gil Jr.'s jealousy. He smashed (or cracked, depending upon whose version you believe) Andy's windshield with a baseball bat. Andy retaliated by coming after Gil Jr. with a gun and threatening to kill him.

Within a few days, a frantic Mrs. Nelson placed a call to her adult niece Lucille Brenna Gould, who was married and living in California. She instructed Lucille to take Gil Jr. in for a few weeks. This was not a subtle request; it was an outright demand as only Mrs. Nelson could make.

"You didn't argue with Aunt Nina," Lucille recalls. "She said Gilbert was running for his life and needed help. In a few days, he showed up at my door."

That impromptu stay lasted several months, until Gil Jr. got his own place in the California desert. Eventually he became a successful engineering supervisor at a major aeronautics company and retired after nearly thirty years on the job.

"I think it's ironic that Aunt Nina took in a whole lot of other people's kids," Lucille observed, "but when she had a problem with her own, she sent him away."

***

My homeless problem raised its ugly head again in the winter of my sophomore year. I had planned to go home for Christmas, after a summer in which we all seemed to once again keep our distance but cohabitate. I called Mrs. Nelson and began to explain my plans for returning to Huntington for the holiday. The response I got took me off guard. Mrs. Nelson told me matter-of-factly over the phone, "It's not a good idea."

I wasn't welcome. I couldn't understand. What I had done wrong? As it turned out, my crime, as told to me by Darren, was that I hadn't been home to help around the house and so I was not welcome anymore. I was confused but hid this from my friends and made up an excuse why I was going to stay at my sister's house. The truth hurt.

Thus, after 1979, I never spent another Christmas at the Nelsons' house, leaning on Rose Ann for refuge during holiday and summer breaks for my last two years at college.

Christmas had been a time for celebration: festive decorations, funny impromptu plays at the top of the stairs and a lavish feast shared by all. Now I was grasping for something to hold onto, and I was truly alone. There was nothing to celebrate and no one to share my feelings with.

I kept asking myself, "Is it really all gone?" while knowing the answer full well.

Undeterred, I buried my head and blocked it all out with my studies and a girlfriend named Diane. I stayed at Franklin Pierce College for four years and did pretty well academically, graduating with a double major in English and Dramatic Arts in 1982.

15

THE OUTSIDERS

Once the Nelson family began to fall apart, we foster kids struggled with who we really were and who we now "belonged to." The honest answer was "ourselves," but we didn't see that until later in our lives. It took getting kicked out of the house to truly open our eyes.

It was bad enough to have to deal with the loss of yet another set of parents. It was even worse to have to explain our dysfunction and emotional hardship to our girlfriends, boyfriends, and spouses. We couldn't see objectively until our reality was held before a mirror, and that was our "significant others."

Sensing her loosening grip, Mrs. Nelson used Soviet Premier Nikita Khrushchev to get her point across.

"Khrushchev said, 'We can only be destroyed from

within,' and he was right!" she'd say, making sure to invoke his name each time an issue or dispute arose involving someone outside the house. Of course, Kruschchev never actually said that, but the fear of Russia taking over the world was shared by many Americans back then. It worked on us.

However, unencumbered by the baggage of our experiences, these "strangers" Mrs. Nelson so feared saw through our Pollyannaish illusion of a model family life. Bit by bit our "family" was becoming exposed for others to see. They couldn't grasp why we didn't just move on and forget the Nelsons.

"They're not your parents," my wife would say, consoling me after yet another negative comment from Mr. or Mrs. Nelson. Or maybe they didn't acknowledge my kids' birthdays that year. Or ever.

But for us kids, it just wasn't that easy to let go and release years of devotion. We dutifully remembered that Khrushchev quote.

So, for Mrs. Nelson it had to be us-against-them or nothing. Our friends, partners, lovers, and spouses were the enemy; people to be held at arm's length and only partially trusted. A glimpse inside the Nelson way of life was like looking into a kaleidoscope filled with a labyrinth of emotions. It made you dizzy after looking for any length of time. Because of this, we never wanted our partners to look too closely. We were scared to let them see the real truth. Who wants to be involved with a family like that?

If Mrs. Nelson's biggest concern was that outside influences would have a negative effect on the family, her fears were justified. These outsiders—all smart, reasonable people—*were* making us all take a critical look at the reality of our situation. And they had a point: individual respect was sorely lacking in the Nelsons' house.

Spouses couldn't be trusted because she couldn't control them, that's how Mrs. Nelson's mind worked. She had no say in who we chose to be with, so any one of them could ruin everything she had conjured over decades. There was no way to be sure who.

She devised a test for the new females: she made them work around the house to see how they held up. With a little effort, they could be molded and brought into the fold. Mr. Nelson would corral the males.

A few, like my wife, hesitated to volunteer. Once Janet was washing the dishes after a meal at the house and Mrs. Nelson came over to the sink and shut the faucet off. Janet turned the water back on and Mrs. Nelson asked her to walk away from the kitchen sink. It was a moment that solidified Janet's distaste for the Nelson way of life. And it was a test Janet failed.

"Are you paying the water bill?" she scolded, which caused both Janet and I to freeze. I was drying the dishes, like old times. "Water doesn't grow on trees."

When we were younger, she would watch to see if we kept the water running for more than five minutes. I knew that water didn't grow on trees because Mrs. Nelson literally told me that hundreds of times. Probably from the day I arrived at her house.

She never liked Janet because Janet wouldn't do chores after that. And the same went for Andy's wife, Barbara, who wasn't fond of folding twenty pairs of boys' underwear three times a week.

Complying with Mr. Nelson's demands was easier for the males who joined our family. The guys were typically eager to build things or go fishing in the morning with him, even if it meant hanging a new garage door or winching an engine out of an old car in the afternoon.

Make no mistake, whether they liked it or not, to be welcomed by the Nelsons, they had to put in the time. And we foster kids were caught in the middle, between the ones we now love and those we used to love.

Our significant others thought it was nonsense to put up with a woman who had such a high opinion of herself. The fear of outsiders led to some embarrassment among us kids, and more than a few spousal disputes, Janet and I included.

"Michael, she never remembers your birthday, or even the names of our kids," my wife would correctly point out. "Why do you even care about this woman?"

"Because she's my mother," I'd defensively answer, trying hard to convince myself. I wanted this family relationship for my kids, so that they could enjoy grandparents from my side as well as my wife's. And besides, to me, Mrs. Nelson was the only mother I'd ever really known.

"I want them to know who my parents are," I said.

"That's never going to happen," said my wife, as diplomatically as she could muster.

I instinctively resisted her negatively, but she was right. "The Nelsons are not your parents."

***

Ironically, it was Barbara, one of those outsiders, who saved our Christmas Eve and gave us all a new place to go when Mrs. Nelson stopped hosting us at the Huntington house. After attending the first few years, I didn't go to Barbara's house for several years, as I had moved to upstate New York and was beginning to make new Christmas memories of my own many miles away.

However, once my kids were grown, I came back to Andy and Barbara's celebration. It's where I satisfied a larger familial need. Uncle Al and Aunt Arline Alifano became annual guests, along with their kids Alison, Robin, and Richard. Due to strained relations between Mrs. Nelson and Aunt Arline (who was constantly questioning Mrs. Nelson's ability to adequately take care of so many kids), the Alifanos had never come to a Christmas Eve at the Nelsons' Huntington house as long as I was there. I don't think they were invited.

To this day, Barbara still hosts the annual holiday gathering and prepares most of the food. Melody usually contributes creative deserts—like little mice made out of Hershey's kisses and sliced almonds. Sometimes we all physically get to her house, some years we don't. Yet we all manage to wish each other a happy holiday somehow. We stay connected.

In the end, the dreaded outsider didn't come inside and ruin everything, as Mrs. Nelson had led us to fear. Instead, Barbara created a new equally rewarding tradition for us, one that thankfully endures.

***

Weddings should have been a time of celebration, but when each one of us boys got married, it was a day filed with stress, embarrassment, and frustration. This made milestone life events unnecessarily uncomfortable. But not for the girls. Mrs. Nelson helped with preparations for Melody's wedding and fawned over Kim's every marital move from afar. In the Nelsons' house, the girls were always treated better than the boys and it continued in a myriad of ways as we all got older. When it came to weddings, Mrs. Nelson felt intimidated by our female spouses. The females were most resistant to her controlling ways.

Yet, with each nuptial, she was losing a bit more control. For her it was a slow, gradual descent into irrelevance. Other parents of young couples might try to work on liking the in-laws, for the sake of finding common ground between the two families. Not her: no way, no how. She was in charge. Deal with it.

Ask Andy, or Darren, or Glenn, or me. We all have stories to tell of Mrs. Nelson misbehaving at our celebrations. When Andy became engaged to Barbara, Mrs. Nelson told people that his fiancé was pregnant (she wasn't). She also told people that Kim's first husband, Michael, was cruel to Kim as an excuse to whitewash Kim's divorce from him when that was not the truth either.

When I became engaged to Janet, Mrs. Nelson told anyone who would listen that she was furious that Janet was Jewish and not Catholic.

"How could you be so insensitive?" she fumed one day over the phone after I had decided to marry Janet. I hadn't seen Mrs. Nelson as anti-Semitic before, but now I was bombarded with new insight. Growing up in her house, somehow I'd overlooked comments she'd made. She once joked with her friends, after negotiating a lower price for an item at a garage sale, "I Jew'd him down."

Mrs. Nelson attended our engagement and wedding

parties and, to our faces, she offered Janet and I pleasant congratulations. But behind the scenes it was a very different story.

Everyone else in the family knew how she felt about Janet. She told them so. Janet and I felt this animosity from the beginning, and it resulted in some uncomfortable moments, even over the telephone.

Making matters worse for us (mostly for me) was that I felt conflicted yet duty-bound to invite the Nelsons to these events. Janet really didn't want me to. At this point, my relationship with the Nelsons had become strained at best. But I wanted to have "my side" represented at the wedding. So, I awkwardly invited Mr. and Mrs. Nelson (Gerry was invited but didn't come).

"If I *have* to be there, just invite me," she said. "We'll see what happens."

They danced for an extended period, disregarding all other guests while portraying the image of a happy elderly couple without a care in the world. Mr. Nelson was preposterously giddy on the dance floor, lightly gliding with his faux dance steps, as if taken back to his younger days as an Arthur Murray dance instructor.

Despite her dismay at my choice of a wife, at the wedding Mrs. Nelson told me she wanted a dance with her son, for all to see. I relented, as I always did to the Nelsons, and she was queen for a dance, right where she felt she belonged.

After the ceremony, she rarely spoke to Janet or me.

It eventually became clear that Mrs. Nelson didn't tolerate diversity, and she never "forgave" me (her actual word) for not marrying a Catholic—or Andy for marrying a Puerto Rican, or Rose Ann for dating a Spaniard.

***

As all of us can attest that, even years after we left the Nelsons, we were still drawn to that house on Bryant Drive, powerless to deny its charm. I personally couldn't shake an obsessive curiosity about what the Nelsons were up to. In my mind, I still couldn't understand why I was let go and sent careening into the world with fingers crossed and eyes closed. In my mind, although I was physically detached, I still belonged to this mess of a family. It's hard to put the hypnotic appeal it held into words. I just had to see it again. It was where I grew up, after all.

One winter day in 1995, Mrs. Nelson unexpectedly invited all of us kids to come and enjoy a holiday together again.

"Let's do it for the kids," said Mrs. Nelson. She was talking about the "grandkids."

After having not seen the house for ten years, I was surprised by the invitation, which was delivered by Melody in a phone call. I was inwardly excited, none-theless. My nervous leg began to instinctively shake. Feeling that bewitching pull, I hesitantly drove to Huntington with my wife and two young kids in tow. Rose Ann came with her family, and Darren with his wife, and Melody with her twin boys. Andy was there with his brood as well. Gerry was there, but Kim and Gilbert Jr. were living separately in California and did not attend.

Disappointingly, and we all agree, it was not the same. We should have seen it coming, but we didn't want to. The house seemed smaller; Mr. and Mrs. Nelson appeared tentative, a lot older and frail; and there were boxes and piles of papers everywhere. The place seemed like an unkempt museum, frozen in the 1970s. It could have been a scene from the movie *Grey Gardens.*

There were boxes of old papers from our early school years, tax documents, letters and holiday cards to and from us kids, and a variety of unknown contents. All of it was now worthless and in the way.

We all walked around aimlessly that entire afternoon trying to find a familiar place in the high-ceilinged living room, which now had boxes covering nearly every bit of floor space as well, right up to that beautiful sandstone fireplace. We ate at the dining room table, which carried so many good memories, but the walls around us were covered in odd religious slogans.

Mrs. Nelson had Gerry set up a small artificial Christmas tree in the center of the living room, like the big one that stood so triumphantly before. But it didn't have the same glow, the light that always gave us such joy throughout the holiday season—even when things weren't actually going well in our lives. My depression was no match for that warm glow. Now it was replaced instead with hastily strewn lights and holiday ornaments, many handmade by Mrs. Nelson for effect.

In the end there was nothing concrete to embrace or spark a memory, just a few whispered stories about how small and old everything looked. Even pictures of a young Gerry and Gilbert Jr. that hung on the wood-paneled walls for the entire time we lived there were slightly askew and covered in cobwebs.

"They are too high to dust," was the excuse. That used to be Glenn's job.

We left that day and collectively agreed without speaking that while it was entertaining being back home, we had witnessed an era gone by. Here I was, ten years removed from living there, and I still longed for it to be mine. It was someone else's house now. After all of the years that I had felt sad for being pushed out, now I didn't want to get back in. I didn't belong there.

That was the last time I saw the inside of that house.

***

By the late 90s, most of us kids, whether with our spouses and children or alone, were no longer invited to the house. Melody visited occasionally, but the rest of us were told to stay away with an array of excuses like, "We're not feeling up to visitors today" or "You can't come in and bring your infections with you." Mrs. Nelson simply didn't want to see any of us, at all, end of story. The relationship had run its course, whether we liked it or not. We had all experienced this type of emotional falling away before, when we were young, in one form or another. Here it was again. I knew the feeling and the dry irritation it left in my throat. So, too, did Andy and Rose Ann and Kim and Melody and Glenn and Charles and Darren.

After a while we got numb and just went with it. *Ok, I'm not loved today, deal with it!*

This absence of paternal grandparents was difficult to explain to my own children, so I simply said that they were my foster parents and meant nothing more. I told them my real mother and father had died, long ago. Strangely, death, with its unique finality, made matters of the family easier to understand for my kids. They were not told the entire story.

Everything related to the Nelsons became uncomfortable, so my family began to disassociate. We moved up north and raised our children in the country town of Greenfield, NY. Mrs. Nelson only spoke to our kids when we ordered them to "get on the phone with your grandmother." I always initiated the call.

And they'd ask, "Who?"

Mrs. Nelson initially communicated with Andy's two children (who were given the Nelson name) and Kim's daughter when they were young, but as with many things at the Nelsons', no real or lasting connection ever formed. Sadly, in her later years, Mrs. Nelson had no interactions with any of our respective kids. There are now more than a dozen grandchildren she never got to know.

With her large "Cheaper by the Dozen" family now scattered, her past behavior caused most of us kids to look elsewhere for love. That's exactly what she feared all those years, that we'd stop needing her. Hers was a tough love. Yet, it might have been our main attraction to her. As kids, we all wanted to be loved, but she thrived on the power of being needed. Helping the poor and desperate, maybe that was her mission. Frustration was her way of showing love. In the end, aggravation was all she had left.

While she resisted the notion of being "destroyed from within," ironically, she was the true reason the family came apart. Mrs. Nelson's mantra turned out to be prophetically damaging to herself. It wasn't our "other" mothers or fathers, or spouses, or a state agency, or any other outside force that caused the Nelson experience to disintegrate. We were a seed she planted but neglected to water.

Eventually she came apart mentally, devolving into a

frail religious zealot who watched satellite TV-delivered Catholic sermons daily. She became an extremely right-wing, adamantly pro-life conservative who loved Rush Limbaugh and hated *The New York Times* and most newspapers, calling them "trash."

She ended up a homebound recluse whose only artifact from a joyous house full of kids was a fifteen-by-twenty-inch photo collage with one picture of each of us. When Andy last visited the house, it hung on a wall behind a stack of boxes, gathering dust and barely visible. He took it home and later gave it to me.

The frame is sturdy and worn, with each photo slightly askew. It's a fitting souvenir.

16

WHAT HAPPENED TO "US"?

Undying emotional attachment becomes unhealthy when it begins to disrupt your life, when it forces you to do and say things you know in your heart are not reasonable, but you do them anyway. The line between healthy and unhealthy connections can be hard to figure out, however, especially if you don't have a precedent for a nurturing relationship.

This explains why, despite all the rotten things we endured there, leaving our disrupted nest, the Nelsons' house, was not easy. As a foster child you learn to follow rules. When those rules are eliminated and you are on your own in the world, it can both freeing and terrifying.

Living with the Nelsons also affected our personal

journeys. Most of us did not go on to college, and personal relationships were tough to navigate. Marriage was particularly challenging: Andy and I are the only ones still with our initial unions intact. Everyone else is on their second or third go-round. For all of us, the patience to develop trust and a lasting emotional bond in our own lives has been hard to muster.

Studies show that the most common diagnoses of children in foster care include Post-traumatic Stress Disorder (PTSD), Adjustment Disorder, Anxiety Disorders, Depression, Oppositional Defiance Disorder (ODD) and Attention Deficit Hyperactivity Disorder (ADHD). Collectively, we kids exhibited all three of theses at one point of our lives of another, which made for a complex stew of interactions, miscommunication, and more than a few curse words—often accompanied by incoming projectiles. Back then (late 60's to early 70's), foster care kids weren't routinely tested, so who really knows for sure? The challenge was addressing these and other "conditions,"— brought on by the indecision and disrespect in our lives— and maturing into well-rounded, confident people.

It was difficult and achievable for us, but the acronym for our shaky condition would have had a lot more letters.

What became of us then, after leaving the Nelsons' household, is a series of different storylines that are all equally circuitous—fun, tough, frustrating, triumphant— routes to the same destination: our new family.

Like gradually retreating ripples, we began to move away in small distances, together but apart from each other. Andy was the first to go, then Rose Ann, then me, Kim, Melody, Glenn, Charles and Darren. All of us, hesitantly but consciously, peeled away from the Nelsons' house and into the wild, multi-colored yonder.

***

Once released into the world, it was hard to adjust, even to the simplest of things. I remember that on a day soon after I left the Nelsons' house for good, I went to a local market to buy dinner. With so many choices on the shelf, I panicked after only a few minutes and walked out with a box of elbow macaroni and a can of lentils. I can't explain my grocery choices expect to surmise that it was comfort food. It seems a bit strange now. Like a prisoner set free after a long incarceration, it was clear that I had to learn how to function on the outside. I felt like I moved at a slightly slower pace than everyone else and kept most things to myself. I certainly didn't feel the urge to confide in anyone. I was hiding, and everything was terrifying.

I graduated from college in 1982. As I was not welcome at the Nelsons' house anymore, upon graduation I went to live with my sister in New Paltz for a short time before moving with two of my high school friends, David and Steve, into a small one-room studio apartment in New York City. We had all graduated from college and were ready to take on the world in our own ways. I had ambitions to be a comedic playwright— my inspirations were Neil Simon and Woody Allen—but soon found that I couldn't make a living at it.

I next hit on the idea of being a comedy writer for television (writing for NBC's *Saturday Night Live* was one of my ambitions), and subsequently I began performing stand-up comedy all over New York City. I created a character named Mort Meek, who was described in a positive review by a critic for the *New York Post* daily newspaper as "a poor schnook looking for a girlfriend."

As a precursor to Pee-wee Herman, Mort Meek was a nervous nerd who wore horn-rimmed glasses, a big bow tie, slim green pants (hand-me-downs from Gil Jr.) that were clearly too short, and a pair of white nursing shoes discarded by Mrs. Nelson. Yes, I wore her well-worn shoes on stage. They were the only funny-looking shoes I had. Mort was a hopeless romantic in search of love, although not really seeing the world as it really was. Sound familiar?

I try to meet girls in New York but it's difficult to find a smart one. You know, someone you can have a conversation with. I met a girl last week, I won't say she was simple-minded, but if they made a jigsaw puzzle of her brain it would be two pieces.

And:

The girls you meet in New York lose everything. I met this one girl; she said she lost her virginity. So, trying to be nice, I spent the next four hours looking for it. I never found it. So, I took her to a party and told her to stand by the lamp while I got us some drinks. I came back to find she and the lamp were getting along better than she and I ever did.

As luck—and lots of it—would have it, an aspiring doctor named Janet Schwalberg came into my life in 1984, after we were introduced by a mutual friend at a party. We went our separate ways for about a year—I pursued my comedy career, and Janet worked toward her degree as a Doctor of Osteopathic Medicine. We reconnected when Janet came to one of my standup comedy shows with a mutual friend. Janet knew him from medical school, while he and I attended Franklin Pierce together. It is truly a small world. She and several other people came to my apartment after the show, and Janet put her bicycle in my bathtub, presumably to get it out of the way. Not knowing whose it was, and a little drunk, I got angry and shouted out, "Who the hell put their dirty bike in my bathtub?" When it was revealed that it was Janet's, I sheepishly apologized for yelling and we agreed to meet at a NYC street fair the next day.

We got married in 1987 and within six years had two children: Lena and Jacob. Desiring steady work, I took a job in magazine publishing and later became involved in trade publications that cater to the television production industry.

Within two years of the arrival of our second child, we moved out of the city, first to a place called Gansevoort, in upstate New York, in 1991 and later in 1994—when we welcomed our third child, Nathan—to the nearby town of Greenfield, where we lived for ten years.

By the spring of 1994, our little family was complete, with Janet having birthed one child every three years to accommodate her rigorous anesthesia residency schedule. I eventually started my own technology writing and publishing company. I've achieved my dream of getting paid as a writer. It wasn't Broadway or SNL, but I "made a living," as my wife likes to say.

***

Rose Ann's life became more complicated once she was out of the Nelsons' house in the fall of 1976. She received an undergraduate degree from SUNY New Paltz in New York and was a credit shy of getting her master's degree (something she worked hard toward but never finished, and later lamented) when she met and married Thomas Moran. The marriage bore two children—Hollyann and Bartholomew—and lasted about sixteen years but was filled with Rose Ann's infidelities and a shopping compulsion that ruined the family's finances.

If that wasn't enough, Rose Ann inexplicably began stealing jewelry and money from her own kids, which caused a rift between her and her children that was never mended.

"Why would you do that?" I asked.

"I don't know," she replied, and I think she was telling the truth. She was lost.

With her personal chaos affecting everyone around her, she moved out of the home she shared with Thomas and into a variety of private homes owned by strange men—men that no one in her family felt comfortable being around.

"Rose Ann, take your medicine," I'd implore, taking on the fatherly figure she lacked. Literally six months before she suffered a stroke, I tried to explain to her that her high blood pressure was going to kill her like it had killed our grandfather, Michael. The bad choices she was making and too much salt in her diet were just as demanding on her body as chopping down a tree.

"What does it matter in the end?" was her morose reply. "I don't want to live forever, and you shouldn't either."

At this point, she lived alone in a single room in a private house for about a year with few possessions and hardly any money. She moved often due to lack of rent money and no stable job. Despite attempts by me to help her out financially and talk to her on the phone for emotional support, she died lonely and broke. Sadly, in the end, even her own children wanted nothing to do with her.

Worse still, the years of emotional uncertainty and seeing her parents fail miserably at marriage took their toll on her. She couldn't bring herself to say "I love you" to anyone, including me, anymore. I believe it was a holdover from our excruciating past and the string of relationships she had destroyed.

"Rose Ann, I love you" is how I'd end every conversation with her in her final years, but my words were always met with silence on her end. The adversities she endured had taken their toll and, as much as I tried to intervene, I was no help.

She couldn't even say "I love you."

As a result of severe depression and choosing to stop taking her blood pressure medication (which was critical, since she had gained weight and was not eating properly), Rose Ann died on February 3, 2007. Her funeral was held in Hyde Park, New York, and most of us kids attended. They all felt a responsibility to be there, not just me.

***

By 1981, Kim, at twenty-one, had also become fed up with living under the Nelsons' roof. With a home health care certification and fearing that she would end up as a personal nurse to the family for the rest of her life (Mrs. Nelson had hinted as much to her), she decided to go west and join Gil Jr. The allure of Hollywood was a factor, not because Kim liked acting, but because she wanted to see movie stars.

"I'm just curious," she said, with celebrities in her eyes.

Before she left Huntington, a guy named Joey asked Kim to marry him, but with her mind set on moving in with Gil Jr., she said no. As a couple in California, Kim and Gil Jr. lasted about eight months.

Never one to mourn a relationship, Kim soon began seeing a man named Michael, with whom she had a child, Tristan. They married in 1985 and were together for a few years before Kim, while she was still married, began dating a guy named Stephen. Stephen and Kim did not marry—although they had a daughter together, Brittany. As an aspiring actor himself, Stephen managed to get Kim a few paid acting parts as an extra on television shows like *Twin Peaks* and *Rescue 911*. Kim also starred in a short music video for the song "Bad Little Suzy," produced by a local amateur band. In the video, she drives a car, flirts with some bad guys, and slaps one of them. This, too, was set up by Stephen. Unfortunately, the video was never aired anywhere, although Kim still has a VHS cassette copy stashed away somewhere.

Within a few years, Kim, Michael, and Stephen all went their separate ways, leaving Kim to hold down three jobs to support herself and her two children alone. Later, Kim married a vending machine repairman named Robert. However, citing incompatibilities similar to those in her previous relationships, Kim's second marriage lasted just a few short years as well.

While Kim had a hard time committing to the men in her life, she always took care of her kids. Unlike her own natural parents, she was determined to keep her children out of foster care, and she succeeded.

"I was determined to give my kids stability in ways my parents never did," she said. "My real parents were alcoholics, but after I left the Nelsons, I never drank and still don't to this day. I was never going to send my kids away, like what had been done to me. I changed everything around."

Today, Kim's children, Tristan and Brittany, are wonderful, productive adults (Brittany is now married with a child), and despite years of difficult situations and unpleasant experiences that required incredible determination to survive as a single mom, Kim is now very happy. She's married again, to a guy named Tom. Kim is a true survivor, and always has been.

However, I don't think she's ever seen a real movie star in person.

***

Although Mr. Nelson said, more than once, that Melody wasn't as pretty as Kim—the undisputed favorite of the Nelson household—Melody carved out her own way by working multiple jobs and attending a community college after she moved out. Her poor eyesight and limited hearing didn't make things easier, but she overcame it all and moved forward with her life.

In 1985, Melody met a local man named Robert. Within a month, he moved into her apartment in Huntington Station, NY, and they were married a year later, on

October 16, 1986. By 1990, with few options and low-paying jobs, they moved back to the Nelsons' to save money for a house of their own. On October 8, 1993, Melody and her husband welcomed twin boys (Robert Jr. and Patrick) to the family. They were living in the downstairs part of the Huntington house, but Melody was determined that it wouldn't be forever.

Of course, Mrs. Nelson always had an ulterior motive for her random acts of kindness. As part of the cost of living there, Robert was "encouraged" to help Mr. Nelson renovate the downstairs level of the house into a one-bedroom apartment, complete with a full kitchen and bathroom. Robert and some of his friends completed the project.

The work came out great, but the results caused a big dilemma. The new, small kitchen officially made the Huntington house an illegal apartment, according to the town's zoning rules. Mr. and Mrs. Nelson were told that, because they now had two kitchens, the town could categorize the house as a multi-family dwelling. This was double trouble: first, the street was not zoned for this, and second, their tax assessment would rise significantly.

You'd have thought the world was coming to an end. The Nelsons nervously instructed Darren, by now an experienced carpenter, to rip out the big kitchen in the main part of the house "immediately!" and install plain white cabinets along each wall. Seeing pictures, all of us kids wondered what was going on. We had grown up in that kitchen, complete with an old table with wooden bench chairs along each side that held seven or more kids and two adults at any one time. It was now all gone...and sad.

Who would want to live in a house without a main kitchen? Two people who were beginning to lose all sense of normalcy, that's who. So, Mr. and Mrs. Nelson, along with Melody and Robert and their two boys, shared the same small downstairs kitchen. Melody and Bob paid rent to Mrs. Nelson every month for two years until they moved out and got their own place in West Babylon, New York.

A few years later, in 2004, Melody divorced Robert and went on to raise her two sons as a single mom. She worked two jobs and didn't take a handout from anyone. I offered several times. She had become proudly self-sufficient.

Melody was always strong like that, in every sense of the word. She became a great cook and baker, too, due to all those years working in the kitchen with Mrs. Nelson. Like Mrs. Nelson had stanchly taught her, Melody can make anything taste good.

She was always the most patient among us and stayed levelheaded through the ensuing years, disappointed by the Nelson experience but never growing negative. She continued to visit them from time to time, but never stayed long. While some of us had become detached from the Nelsons, Melody was always there to help out when the Nelsons needed her. And they, including Gerry, relied on her often. In fact, she was the one the Nelsons called upon when they became ill. Perhaps that's because they knew Melody would never say no.

Grown and with kids of our own, most of us turned our attention away from the Nelsons, but Melody stayed around. It's not exactly clear to even her why, but Melody always came when they summoned. It was part of her good nature and, she says, "gratitude."

Today, Melody works as a clerk (and sometimes

activities director) for a senior citizens' complex on Long Island, arranging parties and hiding the metal knives and forks so the once-wealthy but now borderline-senile men and women don't steal them.

"What is it about old age and silverware?" Melody jokingly asks.

Her boundless creativity shines in every paper napkin centerpiece or fashion show she puts together. The parties she coordinates, complete with loud music and evening-wear models using wheelchairs and walkers, are all the rage among the seniors there.

As a credit to her determination, Melody's two baby boys grew up to be police officers in New York City and the surrounding area.

***

In 1979, with Melody, Kim and I out of the house, Glenn worked odd jobs around Huntington and throughout Long Island while living with the Nelsons. He drove a delivery truck for a time before enrolling at a local community college, SUNY Farmingdale, where he earned a two-year degree in agronomy (soil conservation) and architectural design. His choice of study is a bit ironic since Glenn always hated weeding the garden when we were younger. "This is grunt work!" he'd complain, then move on to the next unwanted weed.

In 1980, Glenn moved in with Mrs. Nelson's sister Rose, the abusive foster mother, in her Smithtown, New York, home. He could have lived in Huntington and commuted about thirty minutes, but he chose to get out of the Nelsons' house. His excuse was that it was closer to the school he was attending. However, like the rest of us older kids, he was done living under the Nelson's random and outdated concoction of conditions.

After graduation and unable to find employment, Glenn enlisted in the Air Force in 1981. It was during his time living and hunting in the woods of Shreveport, Louisiana that he picked up a hint of a "good ole' boy" southern drawl, which has stayed with him to this day. He met a fellow enlistee named Penny in 1986; they married and had a daughter they named Chelsea. Glenn and his new family visited Mrs. Nelson a few times but were not comfortable and never stayed long. Mrs. Nelson liked Penny, but the feeling was not wholly reciprocal.

In 1990, while stationed at the Morón Air Base in Andalusia, Spain, during the first Gulf War, Glenn met another girl in the Air Force named Vicki Machus. Glenn's job was loading live bombs and other ordnance onto planes, which brought him extra pay. The joke was that he also glowed in the dark.

Penny left the service and moved back to her home in Connecticut with their daughter. In her absence, Glenn and Vicki hit it off. Glenn divorced Penny in 1991, and he and Vicki were married in Detroit, Michigan, with a few friends and her parents in attendance. The newlyweds returned to the military—they were on a vacation leave when they married—and had two children (Auriel and Alexander) while living on the base. They now live in Pennsylvania.

When Glenn left the service in 2002, retiring with the rank of master sergeant after years of working at a variety of Air Force bases—overseas in Germany, Spain, and Korea, as well as stateside in California, Florida, Louisiana, and North Dakota—he was a newly invigorated man. He initially worked as a security specialist at a NASA facility in Cleveland, Ohio, before settling in Pennsylvania and working as an IT security specialist for the Department of Defense. He's got a really important job now with the U.S. Navy, filled with exotic travel and meetings with high-level military and government officials, but he's "not allowed to talk about it."

***

Once Glenn left the house, the "little guys" bore the brunt of Mrs. Nelson's by now violent rage. At fourteen and fifteen years old, they were victims of unpredictable verbal outbursts and physical beatings. More than once, Darren walked into the house after a day at school and was met by wild, swinging punches from Mrs. Nelson. It was always something minor that got blown out of proportion, like Darren forgot to lock the door behind him. Or Charles didn't make his bed in the morning. She was losing her mind, all sense of reason, and it wasn't pretty. All that she had built up for more than ten years was now gone.

This also meant that the ever-fragile Charles was now more exposed to Mr. and Mrs. Nelson and couldn't bear the heat. Whereas Darren suffered physical abuse and beat it back with clenched teeth, Charles succumbed to the emotional abuse imposed upon him, held it inside, and it affected him greatly. He took to hiding when he could and cowering and crying when he couldn't. It's clear now that Charles would never have survived had Darren not been there too. They closed rank and relied on each other in ways they never did before, even playing in the high school band together.

After several of Mrs. Nelson's violent outbursts over the ensuing months in 1979, Charles and Darren began taking every opportunity to stay out of the house. Charles began drinking heavily with friends and also sang in several local rock bands that performed at talent shows. They even won a "battle of the bands" competition. The first prize was money to pay for a session in a recording studio. The band members chose to buy beer and drink it all away instead.

Another time, Charles, feeling trapped and paranoid, ran away from the Nelson house and ended up at our grandmother's apartment in Astoria. Grannie allowed him to stay the night but told him he had to return to the Nelsons. He did, but he didn't stay long, maybe another six months. He called our sister Rose Ann and told her he had to get out.

After leaving the Nelsons to live with Rose Ann, Charles tried attending SUNY New Paltz college for a year but dropped out. Heavy drinking had completely over-taken him, and he struggled with it for many years. The Nelsons never contacted Charles while he was away to find out how he was doing or support him in any way. He was on his own. Charles's psychological problems, which were apparent long before he came to the Nelsons' house, followed him relentlessly.

He drifted for a while before taking a full-time job in food service at the college. He met and married a woman named Crystal, with whom he had two children, a girl named Lakisha, and a boy, Lucas. The couple later sepa-rated and Crystal tragically succumbed to a brain tumor, leaving Charles to raise the kids on his own. Despite his diminished mental state, he has successfully done it—raising two well-adjusted children along the way—with a maturity I didn't think he had in him.

However, his mental demons, which the Nelsons could have helped vanquish if they'd cared to, are never far behind.

During this same time, Darren was sneaking out late at night to go carousing with friends. He chain-smoked menthol cigarettes and acted older than his fifteen-sixteen years. This resulted in a disturbing cycle. He'd get caught smoking cigarettes, get beat, be grounded, sneak out at that same night when everyone was asleep, and return early the next morning before the Nelsons woke up.

When his frustration reached a boiling point, he, too, decided to leave. Freedom called, and Darren listened. Without telling the Nelsons, he lived on friends' couches for a full week, totally abandoning high school. After a phone call with Mrs. Nelson, Darren returned to classes but refused to go back to the house. A child welfare counselor was brought in, and Darren was given the choice of going back to Huntington, living in a group home for foster boys in the process of "transitioning to the real world," or going to a larger boarding school for delinquents and runaways. He was advised by the counselor to choose the smaller facility. Darren agreed, wanting to sleep anywhere but the Nelson house.

One afternoon he was taken from school directly to a halfway house in Franklin Square, New York, where he spent a week. He was then sent to St. Mary's Home, in Syosset, New York, a group home for displaced kids, where there was very little supervision and even less control. He was the only white kid among seventy-four

African Americans and six Hispanics. The inmates literally ran the asylum.

Darren appeared on a local cable TV talk show at the time that profiled St. Mary's Home and the good things it was going for troubled kids. He was interviewed on camera for the show and was portrayed as a "model" resident of the place. He now admits that this was far from the truth. In reality, Darren broke most of the rules and was one of the worst offenders, staying out past curfew, smoking cigarettes, and having sex with the female staff. Beatings, given and received between the kids, were regular occurrences. He stayed there throughout his high school years but never received a high school diploma.

One Thanksgiving Day in 1981, during his stay at St. Mary's and after his anger toward the Nelsons had subsided, Darren decided to visit them, unannounced, with a counselor and two other boys from St. Mary's in tow. This was a brave move, after not seeing or hearing from Mr. and Mrs. Nelson for two years.

When they arrived, Mr. and Mrs. Nelson would not allow them to come into the house. She said they were entertaining and "didn't have room." Darren left dejected.

Soon after that day, perhaps out of guilt, Mrs. Nelson began visiting Darren at St. Mary's once a month for about half a year. She always came alone. Then she stopped coming. She had done her penance, as they like to say in the Catholic religion. Mrs. Nelson was always conscious of how the outside world perceived her, and she didn't want to look like she was doing a bad job of handling Darren, her supposed son.

"I went to see him; I took care of him," she'd say. "I've taken care of him since he was a baby." She seemed to have forgotten about the two years of abandonment and the multiple beatings before that, which preceded her six visits.

After St. Mary's, Darren was sent to another group home, this one in Bayside, Queens. He went to school at Bayside High School for six months, then dropped out and at age seventeen, decided to strike out on his own.

But freedom wasn't so easy. He lived alone for a year in an old car that he had bought for $180, parking at a Burger King restaurant and taking showers with a hose at a nearby gas station. With no insurance, no driver's license, and no registration, he was pulled over by the police after trying to outrun them in a high-speed car chase. Although he wasn't doing anything wrong, his tail lights were not working. Darren spent that night handcuffed to a chair in a police station holding cell, his head bleeding from a cut that he's still not sure how he got.

Darren also worked as a bouncer at a local bar. He claims he nearly killed a guy in the men's bathroom by smashing the inebriated man's head against the urinal with such force that the porcelain cracked. He did it to press the bar owner for a raise in pay. He then moved in with Margaret, a former receptionist at St. Mary's. She helped him get back on his feet when he really needed someone, but the relationship didn't last more than two years.

In 1986, at age twenty-two, Darren married a woman named Joanadelle. With money tight and having nowhere else to go, Darren went to Mrs. Nelson and convinced her to let them live together in the Nelsons' house. The times had certainly changed for Darren, having to swallow his pride and move back in, but living on the street was a lot tougher than he imagined the second time around and he had a wife to take care of now.

"It was not an easy decision," he says now. "We really had no choice."

Surprising everyone, Mrs. Nelson welcomed them in and made sure everyone was aware of her charity by randomly calling Melody or Kim to relay the news to the rest of us. Darren had tried the outside world and was coming back. Was she hoping we'd follow?

As an accomplished carpenter by this time, he reached an agreement with the Nelsons that he would complete projects around the house in lieu of paying rent. During that stay in Huntington and prompted by Mrs. Nelson's unrelenting nagging, Darren removed the main kitchen (with materials and labor paid for out of his own pocket) and performed a wide variety of carpentry and other manual tasks around the house. This arrangement lasted eight months. Things became strained over Darren having to pay for all the materials in addition to providing his seemingly unending time and effort.

When Darren decided to leave, again, Mrs. Nelson became enraged, stating, "You told me you were going to be a live-in carpenter." Darren emphatically disagreed and left the Nelsons' house for good.

He unfortunately broke up with his wife four years later, in 1990, when they were living in their own apartment. He soon met a woman named Tonianne Desiderio; they married on November 20, 1994.

By this time, with a successful carpentry business, Darren didn't want a relationship with the Nelsons. His mind said he was finished for good, but his heart sang a different tune. When he got married to Tonianne, he felt that irresistible urge to reconnect. He wanted his side of the family to attend, so he invited us all, including Mr. and Mrs. Nelson. Like my wedding, Mrs. Nelson made a spectacle of herself by not speaking to the bride through-out the celebration and left without saying goodbye.

Darren and Tonianne welcomed a daughter, Chey-enne, on April 3rd, 2000 and all of us kids were happy for him. However, the Nelsons expressed no interest in his daughter. They never acknowledged her ensuing birth-days or shared in special milestones. As it had for my kids and me, it hurt Darren deeply.

Since infancy, he had seen them as his parents, now they were shunning him. After all Darren had done for them, with them, and because of them, it made no difference. Like the rest of us, he was no longer needed. Although, it took him many years to realize it.

***

After minimal contact with anyone but Melody (in person) and Kim (on the phone), things on Bryant Drive grew more desperate. Mr. and Mrs. Nelson were now hermits in an upstairs bedroom of an unkempt house with virtually no kitchen, and Gerry was hanging out in a small woodshed on the side of the house. This was the same shack Glenn and I had recovered from someone's property and erected in the yard many years before.

The reason given by Mr. and Mrs. Nelson for Gerry's crazy living conditions was that he had begun chain-smoking cigarettes. Mrs. Nelson, who had been battling a lung infection, felt the secondhand smoke would worsen her condition. This fear was perhaps exaggerated because her sister Marie contracted an eventually fatal case of emphysema in her mid-thirties, brought on by early smoking, which required her to rely on an oxygen tank her entire adult life. So, lung disease frightened her.

Gerry slept in a bedroom in the house (the same bedroom Glenn, Charles, Darren, and I had been kicked out of years before) but spent a good part of his waking hours watching TV and chain-smoking cigarettes in that shed. There were no windows in the shed, and electricity was supplied via a long orange extension cord coming from the house.

Eventually, with their health failing, Mr. and Mrs. Nelson moved their bedroom furniture to the lower floor, now too frail to walk up that once-magnificent staircase. The house was being turned into an infirmary. All of it—the furnishings, the fond memories of holidays and talent shows at the top of the stairs—was stuck in a dusty time warp. Time, and us kids, had marched on, but Gerry and his parents were stuck in purgatory.

As the Nelsons grew older and sicker, Gerry became their main caregiver. He lived upstairs while his parents lived downstairs. He continued to call Melody, and only her, to ask advice about his personal relationships, talk about the ingredients in a recipe, or seek help in the care of his aging parents.

***

Despite her failing health, Mrs. Nelson continued to defiantly reject us and claim that we lacked gratitude for all she had sacrificed for us. The guilt was her remaining leverage, or so she thought, but our relationship with her was different now. We simply didn't feel the strong obligation we once did.

The sheen of the Nelson family life was now tarnished with time and neglect, until finally the emotional rift was beyond repair. With Mrs. Nelson, it had always been about outward appearance. In her mind, she was a saint for raising poor kids and giving us a home. And she did that; but in her own selfish way, designed to sway public perception (and money) in her favor.

Razzle dazzle 'em. That's how she lived.

17

LAST RITES

Despite all of the difficult circumstances we had endured, whenever there was a "family issue" we all came running to lend support without having to be asked. Mrs. Nelson's funeral was such an unspoken obligation. Outsiders couldn't understand this powerful, irresistible, guilt-ridden attraction to the Nelson family. But for us kids, there is no disputing the truth: the Nelsons pulled us out of our personal hells, and we had a lifelong debt to repay.

That's why one day, after nearly three years of complete Nelson silence—and twenty-five years after I had left the Nelsons' house—I heard from Melody that Mrs. Nelson was in the hospital suffering from respiratory disease. I initially told myself to stay away, but hesitantly, I went to see her. My wife refused to join me. Emotionally,

I had no control. Something inside my heart, at its very core, dragged me there. So, I dutifully showed up.

I walked apprehensively into the intensive care room at Huntington Hospital where she lay close to death. Breathing tubes streamed out of her nose and mouth; her eyes were closed and she couldn't speak. Mr. Nelson was there at her bedside, not saying a word, and didn't get up to greet me. He simply raised his head in acknowledgement. I had not seen either of them in more than two decades, but here I was standing in a room with them alone. I quickly sat in a chair across the bed from him.

There was a long silence, broken only by a series of breathing machines, heart monitors, and the nonstop, furious tap-tap-tapping of my heel on the floor. My mind raced but I struggled for words. I wanted to tell Mr. Nelson how hurtful he had been. How disrespectfully he had treated my wife, my children, and especially me. I wanted to say that I was now the father of three kids and I would never inflict on them the psychological damage he had caused me.

I should have said a lot of things, but he spoke first, without warning and without looking directly at me.

"Mom and I could have moved to San Diego, but we couldn't because of you [Grotticelli] kids."

He said it sternly and with a cold matter-of-factness. Then he looked away and sighed, as if he was relieved to get something off his chest that had been sitting there for a long time. I wanted to vent my frustrations too, but he had beaten me to the punch. Mr. Nelson had out-vented me. After all the years and lived experience, he was still my "father" and I had to submit. I said nothing and it was almost more than my nervous leg could take.

What he was saying was that the whole foster care thing was not his idea. Our relationship was never real for him; this was my confirmation. He was just along for the ride, driven by Mrs. Nelson. I'm sure that's what he would have said had he'd been braver.

"I hear the weather is nice in California," he said, looking at Mrs. Nelson in bed for emphasis. "But I guess I'll never know now."

I was floored by this admission and the abruptness with which it was delivered. I searched for some kind of angry rejoinder and stinging comeback. But I couldn't stand up to him; I could barely breathe. I sank into my chair and my leg began to hammer up and down. Wanting to hide, I covered my face with my hands.

He was talking about an opportunity he was offered by his company, about a year after I came to live with the Nelsons, to transfer to IBM's southern California office. As I had suddenly learned, the Nelsons wanted to move there, but the Angel Guardian Agency would not allow them to permanently move us kids across state lines. It was against the law without parental consent. That permission never came.

After some thirty-five years of kowtowing to him, he was bringing it up now.

As I see it, their choice was to stay in New York or lose the monthly child care payments. Yet, somehow it was my fault that they couldn't move to a sunnier location. I didn't feel guilty but could sense it was being laid on thick. Then Andy, who had been in touch with the Nelsons intermittently, came into the hospital room and the conversation moved to Mrs. Nelson's health. Things weren't looking good for her.

I chose to let the whole wrenching exchange slide, and I have regretted it every day since. I also learned during that visit that the land in Maine had been sold a few years earlier for approximately $85,000. The life-on-the-farm fantasy was gone for good. So was the money that had been taken from Kim, Glenn, and me to pay for it.

***

Mrs. Nelson never came out of the hospital and died on January 9th, 2004, at age 81—or about three weeks after my cruel visit. Things at home became too much to handle for Gerry, so Melody gave up her second job to help take care of Mr. Nelson—foregoing income that she depended on to raise her twin boys. She did it instinctively and without complaining.

Mr. Nelson passed two years later, on June 24, 2006, at age 83. Contrary to the fantasy they had concocted and lived out for so long with our help, Mr. and Mrs. Nelson ended up alone and preferred it that way.

The pallbearers at Mrs. Nelson's funeral included all of her foster boys and Gerry. Andy didn't carry Mr. Nelson's casket. He said his back was killing him, but I don't think it was.

The Nelsons were both buried in modest military style at Calverton National Cemetery on Long Island. For us, carrying those caskets was our duty; we didn't need to be asked. Gil Jr. didn't offer to help carry either casket. Once again, we did the dirty work.

After all is said and done, different people will interpret our Nelson experience as they see it. Those of us who grew up there may disagree on certain aspects of the

Nelson life, yet we all concur that our story has a bittersweet ending. A disappointing finish.

In the end, the way the Nelsons looked upon Andy and, really, all of us (as if we needed yet another sign that our Shangri-La was gone) was undisputedly revealed with the reading of Gilbert J. Nelson's Last Will and Testament. It was the final truth that exposed the lies that came before it. The will was signed and agreed to on February 19th, 2003 and personally witnessed by Mr. and Mrs. Nelson and Gerry.

I acknowledge Andrew Nelson as an adopted child and specifically request that none of my estate or residuary estate ever be distributed or in any way given to Andrew Nelson, his heirs, or descendants. I do this for reasons known to me.

Interestingly, the final wording had been adjusted from a new will signed two years earlier, when Mr. Nelson referred to Andy as his son. That document said:

For reasons best known to myself, I make no provision in this will for my son, Andrew G. Nelson, in that he has sufficient means of his own.

What the words proclaim, in emphatic terms, is the Nelsons' intention to financially distance Andy, their adopted son, from their estate. For the rest of us, the words were worse than a slap in the face because they lasted longer.

Persons who are legally adopted while they are under 18

years of age (and persons adopted after attaining 18 years of age) shall NOT be treated for any purposes under this [Will] as though they were the naturally born children of their adopting parents.

The latter wording appears to be designed to legally shield the Nelsons' two biological sons from having to share anything with Andy. As the will stipulated, everything was left to Mrs. Nelson first and then to the Nelsons' two "natural born sons."

The kids were not entitled to anything monetary or even a sentimental tchotchke. Even after Glenn and I had put a new roof on their house, and Darren remodeled their kitchen, and Kim and Melody had cooked and cleaned for them, and Charles had help maintain their estate. With all of the true grit we had given of ourselves, we got nothing.

We were not previously aware that a will existed, and it was hard to read. There was not even a mention of us in the will, not a single word. We had all had aspirations of one day being adopted, with all the emotional security that might bring. It wasn't money *we* were after.

Andy was the first of us to read it. He had lived his entire adult life using "Nelson" as his surname and had bestowed it upon his own wife and children. Now he was stuck with a moniker that carried negative weight. The stinging yet legally binding words of those insensitive papers ensured that Andy's kids got nothing as well. They had been brought up to believe that the Nelsons were their grandparents. The legalese of the will states clearly that they were not.

***

Angered and hurt, Andy initially contested the will. There was not a huge estate: the Huntington house, worth roughly $350,000, and about $15,000 in cash. He said it was the disrespect that got to him. After the required papers had been filed by Andy's attorney, Gil Jr. angrily countersued him for holding up the disbursement of funds from the estate. Interestingly, Gerry reached an agreement with the respective lawyers to give Andy $10,000, but Gil Jr. refused to relent, saying Andy should not get anything.

"Gerry felt something for Andy," Darren observed. "Wow."

Gerry was coerced by his brother and eventually agreed to cut Andy out.

The day before the case was set to go before a judge, Andy let it drop. He said this last, nagging insult enabled him to see past his aggravation with the situation and gain new perspective. It wasn't all about the money for him.

"I asked myself, 'What am I doing here?'" he said later. "Whatever I get from them, it won't make me a happy man. I could not justify suing my brothers, or those who I always thought of as my brothers."

Andy felt a great sense of relief and could finally move on.

"Not contesting the will was the right decision and the quickest way to wipe my hands clean of it all," he said. "I wasn't happy but held my head up high."

Upon learning that Andy had dropped his lawsuit, Gil Jr. unexpectedly called Andy—they had not spoken previously for a month—to say he was glad that "we were able to end this dispute." He told Andy that he could come to the Huntington house and take whatever he desired, as long as Gil Jr. didn't want it.

His words were little solace to Andy, but, with my prodding, he decided to go. He retrieved a few boxes filled with his military photographs, a wood lathe, and a tapestry made by Mrs. Nelson. He unexpectedly found a box containing eight manila folders, one marked for each kid. Mrs. Nelson had saved a file full of memories for each of us. The folders contained old report cards (even the bad ones), holiday cards we had given her (most handmade), letters she had received from teachers and doctors, school reports and term papers, all dating back to when we were young.

Andy sent the respective files to each of us. Some of us enjoyed seeing the contents of those folders while others didn't care to open them.

He rescued another cardboard box that contained the now-crumbling Black Peter and Catholic Priest sock puppets we had used to perform the Little Christmas plays at the top of the stairs so long ago. There was also an aging pair of boys' underwear with the word "NEWS" drawn across the back, along with a rubber chicken, harmonica, a bow tie, and a goofy-looking pair of fake eyeglasses. All of these things now relics of a happier time.

Seeing the hoard piled high in every room, Andy asked Gerry to let the rest of us come to the house to help clean it out, but Gerry would not allow it. Mrs. Nelson had told him many years earlier that the kids would "steal you blind" if given the opportunity.

About two months after Mr. Nelson passed, and after Gil Jr. had made his escape back to California, Gerry hired a company to host a garage sale. Everything valuable to us was left unsold and discarded with the trash.

When word spread to the rest of us that the house was emptied and up for sale, Darren was angry, Glenn resigned, and Kim nonplussed. I was disappointed. Melody shrugged and barely batted an eye.

"You can't let negative things get in your way," Melody said, in a very Zen way, but really meaning it. "You have to let it go."

18

COMING TO TERMS

Finding closure was easier said than done. Why didn't they like me? Love me? Adopt me? I'll never know. I have the others to consult, but their memories can be conflicting and hazy.

Andy said an icy cold permeated the conversation at the very mention of my name. I now live with that.

"When Dad got sick," Andy now recalls, wishing he didn't have to, "I told Mom I should let Michael know and she said, 'Michael? I don't have a son named Michael.' I didn't know how to respond to that."

When I hear that, I'm reminded of the hurtful phone calls on their respective birthdays, which I made dutifully every year. There would be an awkward silence after I announced it was me, followed by, "So, what do you want?" I knew what to expect when I called—but I did it anyway. My heart said I had to.

Mrs. Nelson would always answer first and quickly put Mr. Nelson on.

"Hello," he said coldly, and then, "You have five seconds."

He then proceeded to literally and very audibly count to five and then hang up the phone.

I had heard and seen a lot with him, but this finished me. I was about thirty-five years old then, and it was the last time I called him. Ever. Five years turned into ten, and, before I knew it, it had been twenty years since I last spoke to him. I once again became a stranger with an empty feeling in my stomach. I long ago stopped fearing the Nelsons might send me back to the orphanage, but I detested getting left behind. I only wish they knew that before they went to their grave.

***

"We all made it out alive," Andy said. "How about that."

How about that, indeed. We are no longer lumped together as a group of foster kids. For all of us, this is a revelation with profound and powerful results. Life outside the Nelsons' house is unfettered freedom and allows you to be your own person. That's a privilege many people take for granted. Do the right thing and live a rewarding life, that's our new mantra.

"It's nice to be taken seriously," Charles would say.

We're slowly but surely moving away from the negatives and all that the past means to each of us. Losing the only stable environment we ever had was disconcerting and kept us all a bit off balance for years. It wasn't fair that it was taken away, but there was no sugarcoating it. Every unlucky foster kid knows what I'm talking about. There are many unanswered questions and lots of feelings that words like "abandonment" and "confusion" don't quite live up to.

***

Despite the seesaw turmoil of the entire experience, I now realize I'm much better off having lived with the Nelsons than if I had stayed with my broken natural family in Astoria, Queens. Or I could have grown up in St. Michael's until I was eighteen, raised with no family at all, and then set free.

The hardest part for me, second only to having been mercilessly pushed out of the Nelsons' house, was having to reveal and discuss this broken life with people like my wife and friends. Both told me I was being taken advantage of and should just walk away, but I didn't want to. I couldn't. While I had been exposed to dreadful things, the words they threw around, like "abuse," didn't describe my experience. "Mistreated" works better for me.

All of us kids can speak to the frustrating inability to explain the importance of the Nelsons and what they still mean to us. My wife can't understand why I went out of my way to make sure I called "home" on the Nelsons' birthdays and on all the major Catholic holidays. There were times, even while picking up the phone, that my hand would shake and I would ask myself that same rhetorical question: Why, when I was being treated so poorly, did I still have a need to call them? I can't explain it, but I made those phone calls.

Observing how Mr. Nelson interacted with us kids in the rough and insensitive way that he did, my wife said it was a shame that I never knew what a real father was, how he put you first, lay his life on the line for you, and roughhoused every now and then. That's the interaction I craved and didn't receive.

At the time, I didn't want to admit it, but I know today that she was right. Charles, Darren, and Melody now say they, too, felt the muddled emotions of building a new relationship while battling that gravitational pull of the Nelsons. As we grew older, interaction with the outside world changed us. There was another way of life out there and it was very appealing. This happens to all adolescents as they mature. However, Mrs. Nelson despised that rite of passage. She craved control and to be the center of attention.

Eventually, for her, both of those things disappeared.

To survive Mrs. Nelson, you learned the real meaning of "her way or the highway." You did what she said or you were out. To her very end, the same stubborn teenager who chose not to graduate high school than give in to her teacher's demands was defiant in her authority and how she thought things should be. Outside opinions were meaningless. She never rolled over for anyone.

***

So, why did we care so deeply? Why are we kids so conflicted about two people who, as we have come to see, made a deal with the state to raise us for a time in exchange for an amount of money? We were income, or more accurately, indentured servants. It was a work farm disguised as a nurturing home. Only the workers didn't get paid; the landowners did.

But it's a bit more complex than that. Together we had many great times—living, working, and playing as one happy family for about a decade. When you're coming from the streets of Queens, that's a dream come true.

The easy answer is that—like Darren, Glenn, Melody, Kim, Rose Ann, and Andy—I needed a father and mother. Everyone needs parents, and Mr. and Mrs. Nelson filled that void. They gave us a semblance of feeling whole, for a time. While they were not our blood relations, there's no denying that in the end the Nelsons continue to live in our blood.

We were vulnerable children and loved them so they would love us back. Every time I look at my old garnet Holy Communion ring, I feel indebted to the Nelsons for giving me a life I would never have had otherwise. If they had not chosen me from hundreds of other unwanted and available kids, I would have lived the life of my four cousins who ran the streets of Astoria, partied hard and died young. I didn't ask to go to the Nelsons, but they cosmically picked me, and I am better for it.

The Nelsons didn't exactly give me the opportunity, but they did set me up to succeed. In gardening terms, they planted the seed but didn't water it enough, so it never reached its full potential. Lo and behold, we grew anyway, into a wonderful bouquet of loving, well-meaning and happy people.

Many of the ill-conceived lessons we learned from the Nelsons helped us become good people, mothers, father, and husbands...simply by doing the exact opposite of what was done to us. In the Nelson house, I was a number, one of the group, without a separate identity. Today, in my own household, I make sure my kids have a feeling of self-worth. Everyone is entitled to his or her own opinion, and everyone's voice is heard and listened to. Sometimes this causes me considerable stress, but my children's contentious spirits usually make me smile later.

***

Om…You Have to Let It Go

All of us have heeded Melody's words in different ways, but we've all come to the same conclusion: we've exhaled the entire Nelson experience from our hearts. It left in a puff of emotions. And we've moved forward, for the better. Some of us are still angry, feeling betrayed and hurt (we can't all be Melody). Others want answers to questions that can no longer be asked, like "Why did you take us in if you weren't going to follow through with the rest of our upbringing?" or "Do *you* remember the happy times?"

Everyone wants to be part of a family, in whatever strange, surprising, unorthodox, messy, logistically challenged shape that might take. For us kids, as long as we remain together and forever in touch, then we have our happy ending.

Perhaps the biggest joy we take from our experience is seeing our respective children interacting with one another like true cousins. That's all we needed, a legacy to pass on, and it's what we got.

Megan, Andy's daughter, got married on October 1, 2011. Some of us traveled over a hundred miles to attend.

Darren was there, and Melody and I. Glenn and his family couldn't make it, but he sent his best wishes. My daughter, Lena, was a bridesmaid for her "first cousin." Uncle Al and Aunt Arline and their kids were there as well. As a natural cycle, the bond is being carried on and our new family is growing, strengthening even.

It was a moment to cherish, as earlier in July of that year, Andy was in the hospital for a toxic gall bladder. The doctor said he needed surgery immediately, but Andy waited so he could walk his daughter down the aisle and traditionally give her away. He danced heartily at his daughter's wedding and we all had a great time. A month after the wedding, he successfully had that surgery and struggled through an intense recovery for weeks.

Lucille Gould, Mrs. Nelson's sister Rose's former foster child, was there as well, marveling at the group of us sitting at the table together. She had flown in from California.

"I wish I had that," she told me, referring to our sibling solidarity. "I don't have anybody from my youth, but you guys have each other." (Lucille does have a wonderful family of her own, which includes her husband, Gerald, and two daughters, Jeanine and Michelle.)

It was then that I realized how successful we had been at forming that elusive family unit on our own. We are more than a group of people brought together through happenstance; we're the envy of others. How remarkable is that?

***

The digital age has allowed everyone to easily keep in

touch, so we often text or exchange email messages. There's no obligation (or bloodlines) to make us care, but we do. Honestly, it's nice.

Fate is a funny thing. There's no doubt in my mind Mrs. Nelson was the reason this happened. She preached the importance of family and it came to pass, just not the way she had originally envisioned. We are a colorful collection of unrelated people who share a common connection. It comes from our shared experience, but she, through sheer will and her seat-of-the-pants philosophy, forged us into a closed unit. Mrs. Nelson taught us to be fiercely loyal to each other and to those we hold dear; not to dwell on negative feelings; to stick up for ourselves; and by all means, "Don't be a martyr."

She also told us to never to be a "gavone," which is Italian for an ill-mannered pig.

"If someone offers you a plate of cookies, take just one," she'd say, "That's it, no more. That shows character and it will make people want to invite you over again."

This from the lady who never let us visit friends, so we never could test out her theory.

Some other bits of knowledge she instilled include: "Don't always be so negative"; "So, you're depressed, do something about it"; "Stick up for yourself"; "Don't' be a martyr"; "You've got to be tough and push through it"; and even "There's no one that's going to help you. You have to help yourself."

Mr. Nelson also taught us how to fend for ourselves, but in a more physical way: mechanical know-how, getting our hands dirty, figuring out problems logically, chivalry ("women always come first"), self-deprecation, and, "One man's trash is another man's treasure."

These were valuable life road maps. Although we didn't understand their full weight at the time, we do now. They are words of wisdom branded deep within us forever.

19

WE ARE FAMILY

So, how do you rationalize being abandoned by your family twice in your life? You acknowledge it, you feel sad about it, and you move on. That's what we all have done. We've weathered loss, sorrow and disappointment, and recovered. I think Mrs. Nelson would be proud, while taking all of the credit.

As we look around now and ponder it all, we have come to terms with our predicament and we are *fine*. Through sheer strength of will, we learned to become functioning adults, without a coach or a safety net. Like learning to swim by jumping into a deep lake. We took that plunge and came back up for air. We forged forward to form our own lives: life's challenges be damned.

"You figure it out." That's what Mr. Nelson gave us.

And we did.

We don't consider ourselves foster kids anymore. We don't even use the term "foster." We are brothers and sisters.

***

Solidarity aside, it's important to note that we all have different views on what it was like to grow up in the Nelsons' house. Sometimes we even have different takes on the same story. Kim will tell you she had a great time growing up there. Charles feels like it was the worst experience of his life. Some have chosen to forget the whole period altogether and talk about it as little as possible. Others fall somewhere in between.

We all agree that things could, no, should have ended more pleasantly and sensibly. Justice wasn't served here; regret was.

Today, when we get together at an event or holiday, we sometimes reflect on how it all ended. We shake our heads and laugh about it, too—some more easily than others. We sit around and commiserate about what could have been our piece of the American domestic dream. We all wanted it, we needed it like oxygen and we came close to getting it. Sure, we have formed a thriving family of our own, but we have never forgotten the one that got away. Now we have each other and the strength in the power of "us." We're all grateful for our motley crew of a family.

Wrapping this story up with a neat bow is a bit like herding cats. There is no easily understood way to describe our Nelson experience, not even a consensus of opinion among us about why it happened the way it did. There's no idyllic picture to be painted, but I was the one who wrote it all down. It wasn't easy dredging up all the fun times that became overshadowed by the heartache. It became a mission I had to undertake.

It's become clear that our early years before Huntington affected us in vastly different yet permanent ways, but the Nelsons added insult to injury. The collective emotional scars have stayed with us, even if we, each in our own way, hide them as best we can. Some of us haven't been able to maintain lasting personal relationships in their own lives, some can't even commit to anything longer than the next day. That comes from somewhere deep.

"We just want to be like everyone else" is the simple yet complex desire I've heard voiced by several of us over the ensuing years. That boils down to the word "family" and all that we came to believe it is supposed to be about. Families are made up in a myriad of ways, but the common denominator has to be unconditional love.

Our story chronicles the convoluted evolution of eight kinfolks who were at best unwanted and at worst forgotten. We've grown together through shared experience, mistreatment, and disillusionment, and held close, if only in our hearts. Given our current separate lives and busy schedules, it can be difficult to get everyone together in person, but we communicate regularly, especially when someone is in need, and as many of us as possible still gather on Christmas Eve at Andy's house. That's a feat to be proud of, something we lovingly embrace.

Individually we are very different people from one another. Our personal paths have diverged. Some pursued education, some learned to be great cooks, a few are handy with tools. So too have our physical attributes. Some of us are half blind, some are short and bald, and others are tall and built like Charles Atlas. In another life, we probably would never associate. Yet, I am as close to and protective of my foster brother Darren as I am of my brother-by-blood Charles. There is no difference. Growing up, we were warned that "We can only be destroyed from within," but we weren't. Despite everything, we solidified that illusive family.

At the end of the day, my story is really one of Paradise found, enjoyed for about a decade, and then lost in a wisp of illusion, confusion, and ultimately the wrenching reality that we were nothing more than revenue-generating warm bodies. We lived for a long time trying hard not to believe that, but I now know it was true all along. I wasn't loved; I was tolerated for my monetary value. We all swallowed whole the Nelson dream: hook, line, and sinker.

And yet, what we went through ultimately shaped our character and made us the resilient, neurotic, and empathetic people we are today. Some people outside the family have a hard time understanding that. And the bad times didn't break us.

Our ties are not made of blood but woven out of emotion and a longing to belong to something bigger than ourselves. No one wants to be alone.

***

So, whenever I'm asked about growing up in the Nelson's house, the best response I've come up with is, "You had to be there." Explaining it is difficult to get right. It's wasn't good, but it wasn't all bad either. We all enjoyed the happy times and weathered the tough ones. Avoiding conflict was the coping method that worked best.

"Out of sight, out of mind" was a mantra we learned, and many times used to our advantage. We didn't have power, or a voice in that household, but we did know how to take a punch and remain standing.

The woman we called "Mom" dreamed of domestic grandeur and a large family, and for many years we helped make her dreams a reality. We were a collection of eight foster kids, all from broken homes we were never returning to, believing in an ideal that was not ours to keep.

We didn't see it at first, but with age came acceptance of the fact that life isn't fair.

At its core, the saddest part of the story is that we were dumped, then discarded again. It's not something to wear proudly on your sleeve. After losing my biological family to dysfunction, I prayed for its return so fiercely and for so long that my entire being became consumed with this yearning and nowhere-to-hide sadness. It clouded my judgements and suppressed my willingness to protest against the injustice. I went silent for so long.

When I came to live with the Nelsons, I thought I was getting another grab at the brass ring of family life. At nine years old, my goals were few: I wanted to feel safe enough to relax, sit in one nice sunny spot, and feel confident that I could enjoy it again tomorrow. I needed people to love and love me back. I wanted to know that it wasn't temporary.

Being born into hardship made Darren, Charles, Glenn, Melody, Kim, Rose Ann, Andy and I stronger people. Our homemade mash-up of a family has seen the bottom of the barrel and, to different degrees, all of us kids have successfully climbed out. Meanwhile, Gerry and Gilbert Nelson Jr.'s privilege growing up became their curse in later life. They have been left without a family or even each other. They live separate lives, rarely speaking to each other, and neither married.

The sad irony is not lost on any one of us. They missed out.

It wasn't easy for any one of us. All of our stories are similar in their heartbreak and took significant fortitude to overcome and persevere. We all found the will and the way. It's the mountain you climb that makes you. The higher and more difficult the ascent, the more glorious the view from the top. Our view is pretty sweet.

In the end, we kids became a family not because of the Nelsons, but in spite of them. But we didn't grow and coalesce from spite, we *got back up and figured it out.* Coming together organically, we found mutual trust and friendship none of us ever imagined. It's truly fantastic. The unlikely alliance we share today is as loving and as strong as any natural familial bond, and, really, all we ever wanted in the first place.

20

BACKSTORIES

Kids are thrust into foster care for a wide variety of reasons. Now that I am a parent myself, I feel like none of the excuses, at the end of the day, hold up to intense and truthful scrutiny. Ask any kid who's been through the system—and approximately 445,000 children live in foster care in the United States every year. We all just want to know "why?" Or, more specifically, why did it have to happen to us?

It's hard to question a system that is trying to do good. It's not perfect and it's not ideal, but foster care is an important safety net that would be missed if it weren't there. In many ways the "system" is very different today than it was in the late 60's and 70's. Yet, the fundamental crisis remains—parents are still giving up their offspring and walking away.

Everyone has a backstory: where you came from, who raised you and the friends you grew up with. Many are sad. As troubled as my young childhood was, the hardship that Andy, Kim, Melody, Glenn, and Darren endured was equally unfortunate. All of our biological parents were able to look away as we got carted off. There wasn't any guilt expressed. If you've never been let go, exposed and unwanted, you can't understand the impotent feeling it causes. We all wish our pasts were different, but they aren't.

Adversity can be an excuse for people not to take charge of their lives. My brothers and sisters faced it head on and slayed their demons.

You've heard my backstory, now here's the rest of the kids' journeys, in the order of their arrival at the Nelsons' home. The date in parenthesis indicates when they were born, to give you a sense of how close in age we were.

Andy (June 7, 1945)

Andrew Jackson Fawcett was the only child adopted by the Nelsons and, as the oldest of the group, wasn't living at the house when I arrived. When we finally met about two months later, he was in full uniform, having just returned from serving with the Air Force in Vietnam. He was extraordinarily handsome and, in his neatly starched uniform, reminded me of Elvis Presley in the photos I'd seen of the King of rock 'n roll during his military stint in 1960. He walked in the front door with an infectious smile and a bag filled with gifts for everyone. I got a plastic chess set with Asian chessmen. It was one of the best things anyone had ever given to me, and I didn't even know how to play chess.

Andy came to the Nelsons in June of 1960 from Lincoln Hall, a state-run home for delinquent boys, located in Lincolndale, New York. He never knew his father or mother. Like me, his earliest recollections of the Nelsons were of trepidation and worry about whether or not this was his last stop on the road to stability. Upon arriving at their home, Andy was told he'd be evaluated for a few days and could stay if he fit in.

In the beginning, Andy tried hard to adjust and soon started receiving a lot of positive attention from Mrs. Nelson, more attention than he'd ever known. This did not sit well with Gilbert Jr. Andy could sense that Mr. Nelson was not as enthusiastic about his arrival and kept his distance. His presence in the young household was clearly Mrs. Nelson's idea.

The same week that he walked through the Nelsons' front door, Andy was given a list of chores to do around the house and an old toothbrush.

"Clean the bathrooms with a toothbrush!" he incredulously read off a list scratched in messy handwriting he was given. "Are you kidding me?"

Fitting in wasn't easy. Andy was a disinterested student and was never forced to work hard at school in his previous foster placements. But Mrs. Nelson was different. She demanded respectability, and that meant getting decent grades in school. When Andy's lack of academic enthusiasm became clear, Mrs. Nelson expended a lot of effort to help him get through high school. The coursework was equally difficult for her, but she adamantly kept the pressure on to do well in school.

"Did you do your homework?" Mrs. Nelson would ask.

"No, not yet," Andy would answer.

"When do you plan to do it?" she'd demand.

"When the cows come home" was one of Andy's smart-ass remarks.

"You need a good smack across the head," she would scold, "then we'll deal with the cows."

Their give-and-take exchanges were ultimately successful, and Andy graduated from Harborfields High School in 1964.

Without any real focus or career aspirations, Andy worked several part-time jobs around town for the next two years, putting money in his pocket but not really getting anywhere in life. Then the war in Vietnam escalated and young men were being drafted. Without telling anyone, he got his draft notice and enlisted in the Air Force. The Nelsons were surprised but didn't stop him. He was getting older and harder to control.

"Make sure you write home," Mrs. Nelson instructed. "I want to see a letter every week."

Her words fell on deaf ears. During his time in the military, Andy received letters regularly from Mrs. Nelson, but didn't write back. He claimed he was too busy but, in reality, he was also not fond of writing letters or doing anything that felt like schoolwork.

"I'm not doing it," he said, and he meant it.

After a few months with no correspondence, Mrs. Nelson sent a sharply worded to Andy's company commander, expressing her dismay at Andy's reluctance to communicate. She dictated orders to a military superior and would not take "no" for an answer.

Her nagging caused the commander to call Andy into

his office and order him to "write your mother a letter." Andy agreed, but never followed through. He'd always done as he pleased. Andy read all of Mrs. Nelson's letters, he later recounted, but never felt the urge to respond.

"I didn't feel like it," was all he said to me. "I told her I wouldn't do it; she didn't listen."

In 1967, one such letter arrived while he was stationed at Lackland Air Force Base. It was a short, handwritten note from Mrs. Nelson stating that she and Mr. Nelson wanted to formally adopt him. In addition to the fact that they had never spoken about adoption before, the correspondence came as a complete surprise to Andy since he was now twenty-one years old, and the Nelsons were no longer receiving payments from the state for him. This was also a new turn of events for the young Nelson family as they had never adopted a child before. He was over eighteen, and thus had aged out of the foster care system.

Andy was given a weekend furlough, and the three of them went before a judge in New York City on June 25, 1968. That day, at twenty-two, Andy became a Nelson, legally taking Gerard as his middle name.

The presiding judge looked down from his high bench and proclaimed, "Son, you should feel very lucky."

"Okay, if you say so," was Andy's smug reply. This wasn't something he had actually considered.

In October of 1969, after a harrowing yearlong stint in Saigon (Ho Chi Minh City), Vietnam, Andy achieved the rank of sergeant and was shipped back to the States and honorably discharged from Robins Air Force base in Georgia. When he arrived home in Huntington, a shiny new red BSA 441 Shooting Star "single banger" motorcycle was sitting in the driveway. It was a welcome home present from the Nelsons. Andy had been saving up to buy a car, so this was quite the surprise. Since Gilbert Jr. had been given a red Hodaka motorcycle months before, the Nelsons wanted to be equitable.

With no experience, Andy rode the motorcycle around the Huntington property for two weeks, crashing into bushes and trees along the way, before passing his road test and receiving his license. (He still has that now-rusted motorcycle in his garage.)

Even with a new mode of transportation and a lot of welcoming hugs, however, fitting in was once again difficult for Andy. After years of carousing in the Air Force, he wasn't willing to abide by the Nelsons' strict rules and early curfews—the same ones he had rejected before he enlisted. He would often stay out late with his friends, which aroused the ire of both Mrs. and Mr. Nelson. After a few months of Andy resisting their rules, Mr. Nelson, prompted by Mrs. Nelson asked him to leave. He was setting a bad example for the other kids in the house. Getting thrown out shocked Andy, but he was defiant and unwavering in his desire to do his own thing, so he left the house and never lived there again—although he visited from time to time.

With nowhere to go, Andy stayed on a friend's couch for a few months before he met a woman named Barbara Spera, who changed his life for the better. She even made him cut his long mangy hair. They started dating in May and they were married a year later, on June 19, 1971. Gerry and I served as altar boys for their traditional wedding ceremony at St. Hugh of Lincoln Roman Catholic Church, in Huntington. They subsequently moved to the east end of Long Island to start a new family.

Kim (August 4, 1959) and Darren (November 3, 1964)

The next kids to arrive at the Nelsons' house were Kim and Darren Newfield, respectively born in Brooklyn and Smithtown. Their parents, Jaclyn Turner and James Newfield, never married or spent a substantial amount of time together. Jaclyn was attempting to reunite with James in 1964 when he imposed the condition that she give up five-year-old Kim and newborn Darren to foster care. So, she did.

James Newfield's version of the story, which he told to Darren years later, is that he broke up with Jaclyn when he found out she gave her kids to the New York State Child Welfare Agency.

Always remaining together, the siblings bounced around in foster care for a year and a half before they came to the Nelsons in 1967. Kim was seven, and Darren was three. Kim was confused about why she was there but happy to be away from the two abusive foster families she had lived with previously.

The parents had a second daughter, Nola, who was sent to a different foster home because she often fought with Kim and caused a variety of problems. Mrs. Nelson had expressed interest in taking in Nola with Kim and Darren, but the Angel Guardian Agency wouldn't allow it.

While staying with the Nelsons, they had infrequent and separate visits with their biological mother and father at the Nelsons' home or at the Angel Guardian offices, where their interactions were closely supervised.

Kim was the Darla to our similarly rough-and-ready cast of Little Rascals. Everybody liked Kim, the way she smiled and how she carried herself. Mr. Nelson often called her his favorite. She had pretty brown hair; a significant nose; and a wide, attractive smile. However, when she'd open her mouth, out would come the salty vocabulary of a well-seasoned cab driver.

Kim never really cared about what other people thought of her. When we were about eleven years old, she was literally the first person I ever heard say, "I don't give a shit." Another popular rebuttal from Kim was, "Don't be an ass."

She was just being herself. Kim was also funny, mostly when she wasn't trying to be, and helpful in any way she could be. She wasn't book smart, but she always out-smarted those who doubted her.

Darren was a sheepish giggler with crooked teeth when he came to the Nelsons' house. He was mostly quiet and fun to have around. When he didn't know what to say, Darren would smile shyly or giggle, and all would be right in his world.

As he got older, Darren developed a nervous habit of picking at his eyebrows, sometimes until there was barely any hair left.

"If you keep picking at them, I'm going to shave them with a razor," Mrs. Nelson would often chide him. By age ten or eleven, he grew out of the habit, but not before receiving a lot of ridicule from the rest of us.

As a very young child, Darren tried to please everyone. If you dared him to do something, he'd do it—and we dared him all the time. He could also take a joke at his own expense, and there were many. For some reason, based on photos from the time, he often wore white turtleneck shirts.

Melody (November 1, 1959) and Glenn (November 11, 1960)

The Keppler siblings, Melody Marilyn and Glenn, were born at City Hospital in Queens to Roberta Polleck. Although their birth certificates show Richard Keppler as their father, it's clear from their appearances that this is not the case. Melody is a redhead with freckles and a feisty temper while Glenn has brown hair and a quiet demeanor. Glenn also grew to be a lot taller than Melody.

Melody and Glenn landed at the Nelsons in 1961, when Melody was two and Glenn a year younger. Both kids saw their mother on monthly visiting days at the Angel Guardian offices in Mineola for several years.

As often happens in foster home situations, Roberta suddenly took Melody and Glenn back to Florida in the summer of 1969, which was her parental right but very disruptive to Melody and Glenn. Glenn returned to the Nelsons within a year, after his mother stated he hated her and she couldn't handle him.

The truth, according to Glenn, was that Roberta and the police detective she was living with—and later married only to divorce—occasionally beat both of them. Once he went so far as to put Glenn in a jail cell for a few hours to teach him a lesson.

"He was as scary dude," Glenn said, "and I wanted no part of him. I didn't get along with anyone in Florida. It was better at the Nelson's house."

Melody was forced to stay with her mother a while longer, but she also clearly didn't want to. Mrs. Nelson tried to intervene but The Angel Guardian Agency sided with Roberta, and Melody was stuck in Florida for over six months. With a mother who didn't pay much attention to her and a scary father figure, Melody pleaded to come home to the Nelsons. There were numerous tear-filled phone calls involved before she returned to Huntington on October 2, 1971. Everyone was happy for her and eager to be rid of the stress it caused.

Roberta had two children before Melody and Glenn, but the collective kids never knew each other and never sought each other out. Melody's dad, Richard Keppler, was listed on her birth certificate as a "nuclear energy drafts-man," but Melody does not recall much about him or his physical appearance. Their mother worked as a waitress at a string of diners and restaurants, ran around with different guys and didn't really like being tied down with kids. So, she threw Melody and Glenn into the foster care system like extra baggage.

Living with the Nelsons, Melody tried her best to look as vivacious as Kim, but with a gap in her front teeth, wiry red hair, cat-eye glasses, and a hearing disability, she didn't stand a chance. When I met Melody, she had hearing aids in both ears but typically she often didn't wear them. This instigated more than a few arguments due to miscommunication.

"Hey, Mel, how do you spell 'tuberculosis'?" I'd ask, teasingly testing her.

"How do I smell what?" she'd say, her bad hearing getting in the way.

"Never mind."

As for those nerdy glasses, Melody says she caused herself to need glasses by crossing her eyes for long periods to get attention until she weakened her optic muscles. It's a story that can't be proved, but the rest of us can certainly see kooky Melody doing that.

She wasn't really into any school sports and rarely played baseball with us boys in the backyard. Her skills were honed in the kitchen where she became as good a cook as Mrs. Nelson, which is saying a lot.

Glenn was slight of frame as a young kid and quiet most of the time. Like many of us, he didn't speak unless spoken to first. And he hardly ever smiled. Every photo we have from that time shows him frowning—at weddings, funerals, backyard gatherings, whatever and wherever. He always looked like he was in a bad mood, but he wasn't—well, not most of the time.

He also wasn't one to start a fight, but Glenn never backed down when confronted. He had a comical expression for whenever something was happening that wasn't to his liking. He'd half-whisper, "That's messed up," and shake his head in mock disbelief. That was about as angry and as loud as Glenn ever got.

ABOUT ATMOSPHERE PRESS

Atmosphere Press is an independent, full-service publisher for excellent books in all genres and for all audiences. Learn more about what we do at atmospherepress.com.

We encourage you to check out some of Atmosphere's latest releases, which are available at Amazon.com and via order from your local bookstore:

Geometry of Fire, nonfiction by Paul Warmbier

Pandemic Aftermath: How Coronavirus Changed Global Society, nonfiction by Trond Undheim

Great Spirit of Yosemite: The Story of Chief Tenaya, nonfiction by Paul Edmondson

My Cemetery Friends: A Garden of Encounters at Mount Saint Mary in Queens, New York, nonfiction and poetry by Vincent J. Tomeo

Change in 4D, nonfiction by Wendy Wickham

Disruption Games: How to Thrive on Serial Failure, nonfiction by Trond Undheim

Eyeless Mind, nonfiction by Stephanie Duesing

A Blameless Walk, nonfiction by Charles Hopkins

The Horror of 1888, nonfiction by Betty Plombon

White Snake Diary, nonfiction by Jane P. Perry

From Rags to Rags, essays by Ellie Guzman

Giving Up the Ghost, essays by Tina Cabrera

Family Legends, Family Lies, nonfiction by Wendy Hoke

CPSIA information can be obtained
at www.ICGtesting.com
Printed in the USA
BVHW070854231120
593966BV00008B/125